Eternal Wave

Tom Norman Dinwiddy

Eternal Wave

JOHN SCOTT HUGHES

Illustrated by
David Cobb, R.O.I.

TEMPLE PRESS
LONDON

By the Same Author

KING OF THE COCOS
ORDEAL BY AIR
UNCLE SAM'S SCHOONER
FAMOUS YACHTS
LITTLE SHIPS
TOLD IN THE WATCH BELOW
SAILING THROUGH LIFE

Edited by John Scott Hughes

MACPHERSON'S VOYAGES
SAILING. By E. F. Knight
THE COMPLETE YACHTSMAN
By B. Heckstall-Smith and
Captain E. du Boulay

Printed and bound by
JARROLD AND SONS LIMITED
NORWICH

IN MEMORIAM
T. N. D.

Acknowledgements

Gratitude is expressed to the Royal Cruising Club for their kind permission to quote so copiously from the logs which T. N. Dinwiddy published in their *Journals*.

Contents

Illustrations

PART ONE
In Sail

1 *Introductory*

A YEAR or two ago, in a book called *Sailing Through Life*, I set out to tell of the vessels in which I had myself sailed, and of some others which had a special interest for me. Referring to the index, I find that the total number of them was ninety-nine.

That my pen was stayed at the ninety-ninth was doubtless a respite for the reader. But it has turned out not unfortunately for me also, because after I had done with the book I discovered a lot of facts about my hundredth vessel, and in the process, such is the kindly way that these things fall out, she has been teaching a few things to me.

My knowledge of *Eternal Wave* is second-hand, from the man who made her famous. But not quite all of it. And perhaps, having started with the first person singular, I may be permitted to tidy-up my own unimportant part in it first.

There was a time, 1938 about, when there seemed a reasonable chance of my buying her from Dinwiddy.

However, the months went by without my being able to raise the sum he asked for her, though it was nothing extortionate, and in the end *Eternal Wave* was bought by Hugh Ruttledge, the explorer.

Then came the War. Within a week I was without a job, without any income, and presently, when the war warmed up, without a home.

After a month or two, which were not without their anxieties, I found myself repeating, though much less light-heartedly, an experience of a quarter of a century earlier; this was going to Gieves on a dark November day to be fitted for the R.N.V.R. lieutenant's uniform.

Service in the Navy, the desk exchanged for a deck, liberated fellows by the thousand; it imprisoned me.

'All those clerks and clerking!' once cried a testy skipper, shaking a walking-stick, at the Port of London Authority building. 'That's what I—hate!'

The only difference now in war-time was that the clerking inside the Port of London Authority was done by the Navy, scores of us, deeper in paper than I can describe.

Without receiving and signing for a thick pad of forms, twenty or more sheets of paper, no shipmaster could move his command one single yard. Alas, to us handing out the stuff—degaussing certificate, routing instructions, black-out regulations, swept channels, sunken wrecks, and goodness remembers what—it could be no concern whether a ship was bound for Bilboa, Brisbane, or Blyth. Nor did it seem much to matter to these Merchant Navy captains, such were their fine manners, good humour, and unshakeable calm.

4

To feel that one might be encumbering men having such awful responsibilities was distressing, and it was not long before such a feeling, working on an out-of-sorts body, for I had lived always unconfined and much in the open air, made me ill; when the all-merciful Providence, to which I turned in my trouble, arranged a change of scene which I will delay describing only long enough to record a sentence heard when two captains were conversing on professional matters.

'When we landed in Gallipoli all we had was a White Ensign, a bottle of Scotch, and a tin of sardines.'

A sort of sub-office of the Naval Control had been set up at Thameside (as it may here be called), where ships were boarded when they reported themselves to be in difficulty, which in the earlier days of the magnetic mine was often enough, goodness knows, though later the situation became yet grimmer.

These boarding missions required some type of boat, a boat's crew, and, as naturally, a boarding officer.

This was the new job, and this was how *Eternal Wave* became mine, free, gratis, and for nothing one might well say, for even her upkeep was provided for in the unimaginably vast sum voted for that spring in the Navy Estimates.

The contingency that brought us two together—when you try to think of the hundreds of ports and thousands of men and thousands of craft—is it not astonishing?

The pleasure I got out of her, foaming up and down and across the river, for like all her sort she shoves up a self-important bow-wave, was immense; and besides the fun there was the fresh air and freedom, and hence returning health and a measure of sanity. For on the river, always with little bits of jobs on hand, one was not stifled with all those *forms*.

Indeed I could only with reluctance ever bring myself to go on shore, but would instead sit about for hours on the low coach-roof gazing at the unending sombre pageant of war-time Thames, and all the while not inattentive to minuter sensations—which have, however, always meant much to me—as, say, the not unmusical complaint of a fender under pressure, the lisp of the running tide, and the slight and intermittent cradle-motion it imparted to *Eternal Wave*.

Eternal wave!

So perhaps it was not altogether without reason that before long the people in the office arrived unanimously at the conclusion that their boarding officer was daft.

But no, not unanimously, otherwise I might not have got wind of it.

Our senior officer was a retired captain, R.N., whose office window overlooked my command whenever she lay alongside. On one such occasion a lieutenant R.N.V.R., my friend the brilliant B. W., was with him in his office. The Old Man had been looking out of the window for some time, when, turning slowly round, he exclaimed, in much perplexity:

'You know, I can't make that feller out. I just

can't make him out. There he is again. Staring at the water. What's the matter with him, eh?'

'Oh I don't know, sir,' said B. W., who never could resist scoring off the R.N. 'He might even be *thinking*.'

One could not avoid noticing in Captain C——, by the way, that he walked painfully, as though his shoes were always hurting.

There came a day (towards the end of my tour of duty at Thameside) when B. W. overheard him at the telephone, on the Admiralty private line. Even from a one-sided conversation it was perfectly plain that he was being offered the command of a battleship.

'Oh no, Percy, not a battle-boat. Though thank you so much. Really I couldn't. You see, *it's my poor feet*!'

2 *Tom Norman Dinwiddy*

THIS book is not intended to be about my own sailing (such as it has been, and about which elsewhere I have had my say), but rather about T. N. Dinwiddy, owner of *Eternal Wave* and other craft—a worthier theme.

And even here I scarce dare trust myself to steer a steady course, too well knowing it to be a weakness of mine to luff up or bear away *out of curiosity*; and so bring in what X did, and what Y thought, and how Z summed up the matter. All this quoting of Tom, Dick, and Harry! But ought it not always to be so when one is in company with one's betters?

Tom Norman Dinwiddy died at his home in Stoke Gabriel, South Devon, on April 20, 1945, slipping his cable with the gentleness which was the first thing noticed in him, and, most likely, will be longest remembered.

Reserved in speech, unobtrusive in his manner,

dress, and bearing, he was modest and self-effacing 'to a fault' as we say. Aboard ship he was pernickety, as some superb seamen are. Everything must always be quite spotless, everything always in its place, everything must always be done just-so. A bit of an old maid, perhaps, to the majority of people—including, for a time, even his devoted paid hand, Eales J. Bartlett—and what is called a 'difficult' shipmate.

In character he was resolute and inflexibly determined, the more inflexible because, for all his gentleness, he had complete confidence in the correctness of his convictions. One might make one word do by simply saying that he was pig-headed. All the same, whatever he undertook that he duly performed, meticulously, exemplarily.

This combination or even confusion of qualities appears to be not uncommon in men who are distinguished adventurers; and Tom Norman Dinwiddy was one of the most courageous and most able amateur seamen of his generation—which claim, recalling however briefly the achievements of his contemporaries, is as high as could be made.

Such facts about his private life as can concern us here may be told in a couple of sentences. After being privately educated he became an architect, and (in due course!) F.R.I.B.A. In the First World War he was a captain in the 2nd V.B. Royal West Kent Regiment, and later a lieutenant R.N.V.R. (Auxiliary Patrol). He was, or had become, sufficiently well-to-do to retire early, and shortly before his fiftieth year he left Blackheath to settle in Stoke Gabriel. He was married, but there was later a separation; there were no children. His will included bequests to the

R.N.V.R. (Auxiliary Patrol) Club, £1,000; and to the
Royal Cruising Club's special fund, £500.

His retirement in South Devon was from the beginning devoted to yachting, sailing all through the
summer months, whiling away the winters with the
model-making and so forth at which he was so adept,
and in planning, with characteristic thoroughness, the
voyage he proposed to make in the coming season.
Devotion, indeed, is not too strong a word for such
complete absorption; and if a man's life consisted only
in the abundance of such satisfactions, none could be
more enviable.

Dinwiddy's extensive cruising was begun in the
sailing yacht *Blue Jay*. Goodness knows the time and
trouble, the thought and care, involved in the selec-
tion of just this vessel. He might have ransacked the
offices of the world's naval architects. What is certain
is that he *must* have studied every modern design. For
the lines were published, in the *Yachting Monthly*, the
winning design of a competition, in November, 1908;
that is, twenty years before Dinwiddy thought of
building.

The designer was Albert Strange. The most
generally-marked feature in a yacht by Albert Strange
is the double-end or canoe-stern, at the contriving of
which he excelled all others; but this was not his only
excellence. Every design of Strange's has not only a
look but also an air of good-breeding, and a kind of
buoyant beauty, which is somehow preserved in the
most neglected boat, so that when you know what to

look for you can tell 'an Albert Strange' anywhere and at any age. Strange was also an artist in the narrower sense, a draughtsman and painter, and he also taught art, at Scarborough, I fancy. But there, one mustn't ramble off like this!

Blue Jay was built by W. E. Thomas, Falmouth, and completed in the spring of 1926. She was a 12-tonner; main measurements being 30 ft. waterline, 39 ft. over-all, 9·6 ft. beam, and 5·25 ft. draught. She had 730 sq. ft. of sail, disposed in the ketch-rig. And since rig is the argument that yachtsmen most delight in it is useful to have Dinwiddy reporting that 'The ketch-rig has proved extremely handy in bad weather, although of course sacrificing something to windward, she has proved fast and well-balanced with almost any distribution of full or reduced canvas.'

Blue Jay had a small auxiliary motor, a 7 h.p. Kelvin driving a folding propeller, of which use was made only under strict necessity.

When Kipling's young man heard the Red Gods calling him to sea, he asked for

> *An extra hand to bale her*
> *—Just one able 'longshore loafer that I know.*

The trouble with the longshore loafer, however, is that he is seldom able because his parasitical manner of living atrophies whatever abilities he may have had.

Dinwiddy did better than a longshoreman when he shipped a young fisherman straight from a Brixham trawler; a splendid nursery for smart fore-and-aft seamen, up to quite recent times, but now, alas, no more.

'My good Brixham hand', was the owner's opinion of Eales Bartlett. 'An excellent seaman who fully upholds the Brixham men's reputation. A good worker and a good cook, and three hot meals a day was a rule that seldom had exception.' (One might add here, though it may not be the place for it, that whenever he could Dinwiddy dined on shore to give the cook a respite.)

Will some think it impertinent that one should wonder what, in turn, the man thought of the master? At any rate, it is a speculation wholly natural to me, more than once a paid hand myself. Besides, the relationship of amateur and professional, above all in a cruising yacht, being so peculiarly intimate—'Oft in danger, oft in woe!'—is extremely favourable to the forming of a just estimation of character.

It is therefore with the deeper pleasure, tempered though it may be with relief, that one finds Bartlett speaking of his late owner in the warmest terms:

'Mr. Dinwiddy was the finest navigator I ever sailed with, and he could endure hardship as well as any fisherman I ever sailed with.

'He just lived for the chart and the sea.

'I would go so far as to say you would have a job to find a man in a thousand like Mr. Dinwiddy. In his own village people knew him as I have described him.

'He was generous, outspoken, strict, and straight.'

There is more, and we shall come upon it in due course; but one would wish to pause a moment on the perfection of that enviable epitaph.

Generous, outspoken, strict, and *straight*.

And here I am reminded of *Tom Diaper's Log*, which I recently read, in which is described the career of a distinguished professional racing skipper. This Diaper, Tom, was one of a family of ten, whose father was that Tommy 'Dutch' Diaper, whom most authorities agree to be the greatest of the great yacht racing professionals. Or at least among the half-dozen greatest, as witness this tribute from one of them, Topsy Miles, when he was talking of his peers—the Cranfields, Gomes, Tom Jay, Butty Parker, Carter, Charlie Barr, Archie Hogarth, 'Lord' John Houston, and Bobby, Tug, Dick, and 'Cook' Diaper:

'These, with their crews, mainly from Itchen Village, were the men who were the admiration of the yachting community the world over and the idols of us Itchen lads.

'Amyas Leigh, standing on the quay at Bideford, was not more sincere in his worship for his glorious Devon than us lads, in our admiration of the splendid men who taught us all we knew. . . . And "Dutch" Diaper, who handled the old *Norman*, the *Sleuthhound*, and Lord Dunraven's first *Valkyrie*, as fine a speciman of a man as I have ever seen; standing six feet in height, weighing fourteen stone, lean as a greyhound, sinews standing out like strands of wire, he cared for nothing breathing . . .'

In the little book by 'Dutch's' son, Tom, we are shown the other side of the medal, with its many and constant anxieties. For the capital difficulty that besets a yacht captain is that the manners of a courtier, the tact of a diplomatist, and the highest professional competency are expected of him by his owner. Great professional skill Tom Diaper certainly possessed. His manners were those of a respectable and self-respecting British seaman—would that such were more widespread. But tact, tact of the placatory kind, which connives that all is well when all is very wrong, tact of the yes-man kind, this Diaper never had and so never used. Hence, it seems to me, stemmed the most part of all his worries; though indeed it was mainly one worry, that of being out of work.

So we have in his pages the picture of one of the great skippers, during the great period of British yacht racing, filling in his time between jobs as a ship's painter in the dockyards, or general handyman in a yacht yard, or even casual labourer. He often expressed anxiety, but he never complained, and this is the most touching thing about his book.

Tom Diaper was what we call, in an unthinking way, an uneducated man. But as his tale unfolds, and as gem after gem of honest thinking and right-doing are disclosed, we may catch ourselves reflecting that the times we live in could do with much more of this *uneducation*.

3 'Blue Jay'

AFTER the launching of *Blue Jay* in the early spring of 1926 her interior was finished off by Dinwiddy himself—'very handsomely', in the opinion of Bartlett, who joined the ship at Paignton in the latter part of April.

All that summer was employed in what might be called a series of shake-down cruises in the English Channel and along the coast of Brittany, both men getting to know the ship, and, as importantly, getting to know each other.

'I knew little of my owner's qualifications, but I soon found out he was very clever indeed. He was a man of few words, but when it came to doing things in general there were times when he was jovial and smiling. I would try to keep it going, but smiles were not too frequent. He always appeared to be solving problems going through his mind.

'I soon found out he had his funny ways, and for the first three months I found his fads boring, and I had to keep it in check. As when we were out one day for a sail and every time we came about the order "Lee-O!" could be heard for some distance around.

15

And once there there was a little more added to it. I went aft to him and this is what I said: "I have known how to trim a jib or fores'l since I was sixteen or seventeen years of age, and don't you call me a damned fool again as one day I will prove to you I'm not."

'And from that day till the day I left him he treated me as I expected of him.

'But if at any time I had shown any unwillingness to be under way at 3 a.m. or any even earlier time in the morning, he would have been very annoyed indeed. Whenever I had to call him he was always up like a lark. About three hours seemed always enough sleep for Mr. Dinwiddy.

'On our first cruise, leaving Hamble at 4.30 a.m., passing the Owers and then Beachy Head, approaching Dungeness a heavy sea began to make, and *Blue Jay* was reefed fore and aft. And now I saw that I was with a very good man, fit to sail with anywhere.

'Mr. Dinwiddy did not like a man to be dull. He wouldn't keep knowledge to himself. He taught me chart-work, and would like to have made me as advanced as himself.

'He said to me one day, "I like a man who can swear in reason, and drink a pint in reason."

'I replied, "One of those things will do me."

'"Which one?" he asked.

'"The driest of the two."

'"Very well", he said. "And don't forget, Bartlett, not to condemn a man for his bad points if he has more good ones."'

During that winter, 1926–7, Dinwiddy planned his first considerable adventure in *Blue Jay*. This was done in the most methodical manner, as was his way in everything, and well beforehand all the facts were assembled—courses, distances, lights, tides, tidal-streams—and noted down on the left-hand pages of the log-book, whose right-hand pages were reserved for the log proper. He preferred to have all courses and bearings in degrees, by the way, rather than complex fractional points, despite respect for old customs of sail.

The objective for 1927 was Orkney. The itinerary was to be as follows: from Dartmouth they would sail up the west coast to the Isle of Man, and from there work up north to Stornoway in the Hebrides, and thence to Orkney, returning down the east coast of Scotland to the Moray Firth, through the Caledonian Canal to Oban, and from there homewards down the west coast once more.

When the time came, *Blue Jay* cast off from her permanent moorings on May 26, and returned to them on July 14, with 1,605 miles on the log, having completed the cruise as planned.

Perhaps one should not have said 'as planned'. For the sea being the sea, and the weather being what it may be, on a cruise of any respectable length and duration affairs can never run in any pattern that can be exactly foreseen. If they could, what would become of yacht cruising?

To begin with, the weather that summer, along the

western side of these Islands at any rate, was the worst for years. The strong winds usually had more than a touch of north in them; and when *Blue Jay* was in Scottish waters it rained almost all the time.

However, before she was half-way to Scotland the yacht was in trouble that might have proved more serious than stress of weather. This was her dismasting when 30 miles south-west of St. Anne's Head. Dinwiddy describes the incident in these words (in reading which we should have it in mind that what for Dinwiddy was a fresh breeze the less hardy of us would believe to be strong to gale, and similarly with state of sea, etc):

'At 10.40, when sailing well in a fresh breeze but not overpressed, though the easterly wind across a swell had made a short uneven sea, *Blue Jay's* mast carried away at the top shrouds. The helm was at once put down, but almost immediately the mast went again at the peak and jib halyard-band, and then by the board.

'The mast was a grown spar, $6\frac{1}{4}$ in. diameter and 31 ft. above the deck, carrying a sail area of only 557 sq. ft. The fracture was "short" and without warning, and I can only think it was a "natureless" spar.

'With some difficulty the wreckage was cleared in the lively seaway, but eventually the spars, sails, and the whole of the gear and fittings were salved and secured, and the mast in three pieces sent adrift, and it was then found that the log-line had, during the drifting, hopelessly fouled the propeller—though the small auxiliary engine would have done very little against the wind and sea.

Dismasted

'A steam trawler hove in sight, and, seeing that the wind being east, with a ketch's short boom as jury-mast and the mizzen, the only other hope would be to sail to leeward and make the Irish coast, I arranged for a tow to Milford Haven where repairs could be effected, and at 13.50 *Blue Jay* was in tow, the estimated position (confirmed afterwards by the trawler's course and speed) then being St. Anne's Head bearing N.E.½N., 30 miles.'

Do not these sentences reveal a good deal of Dinwiddy himself? One cannot say he is at pains to be precise because, as the phrase goes, he was precision itself; and though one may be amused at his mild accusation, as it sounds, against the mast for being a 'natureless' spar (whatever that may be), one must admire the level-headedness and the seamanlike way in which the incident is both described and disposed of.

But here, perhaps, is the place to ask a pause in which to state the difficulty with Dinwiddy's logs.

The reader will have no doubt marked, in no pedantic spirit, Dinwiddy's imperfect mastery of syntax (as in the last-quoted sentence, where it could be read that it was the east wind that had a ketch's short boom, etc)., but this is a mild difficulty compared with the congested, even congealed, mass of dates, times, courses, distances, barometer readings, bearings, speeds, place-names. Slap into the log goes every fact; no variation of emphasis, tone, mood, indeed no thought, feeling or opinion of any kind. *No expression.*

But this is hardly fair; indeed not strictly true. It may have been Dr. Johnson who said that a man couldn't write thousands of verses without producing a good line now and then. And so with Dinwiddy, where an occasional sentence looms out of vague intelligibility, as it were, and becomes vivid and alive for us. Indeed, we may discover more than a few.

Blue Jay was eight days at Milford Haven having a new mainmast fitted and stepped, and when she put to sea again she met such hard winds in St. George's Channel that latterly she had to run for Holyhead—being pooped in the process, though this word is not used in the log, which says, 'Although *Blue Jay* has proved an able boat in a seaway, two successive waves three-quarters filled the cockpit—and at Holyhead twenty-four hours were spent in port drying out the ship.[1]

The next passage was to Douglas, Isle of Man. Under way at five in the morning the yacht turned to windward in a moderate breeze all day, making port at six in the evening, distance 54 miles. This was a fine day. 'One of the only two or three pleasant summer sails of the whole cruise.'

From Douglas to Campbeltown in mixed weather—distance sailed, 148 miles; made good, 99 miles—and a beat up Loch Fyne in a fresh northerly. 'Being Sunday Crinan Canal was closed.'

[1] POOPED: An example of Dinwiddy's understatements. Bartlett affirmed that 'a broken sea *filled* the cockpit', and added that it was the worst sea they ever experienced in *Blue Jay*.

When the canal resumed business *Blue Jay* made an uneventful passage through and was then in those waters whose landmarks have such wild and heathenish but always enchanting names—Ris and Vic Faden, Ashnish, Loch Na Keil, Cuan, Seil, Scavig, to name some on the romantic road to Tobermory, where the yacht was watered and provisioned.

Always strenuous and occasionally grim was the passage northwards among the Western Isles, as these random log extracts show:

'Under way at 03.55 with double-reefed mainsail, No. 3 jib, foresail and reefed mizzen.'

'Wind very strong S.W., and much rain. Anchored off Kyle Akin. Ashore for letters and for dinner.'

'Hoisted double-reefed main intending to sail to Portree, but the wind veered to N.W., strong, with more heavy rain.'

'Off Portree wind N. by E., cold and wet and thick with rain. Ashore for provisions and for dinner.'

'Under way for Stornoway, reefed mainsail, etc. Soon strong puffs of wind came from all points of the compass—reefed mizzen—and then came N. by E. strong and squally with heavy rain.'

'*June 23*. Stornoway. Ashore in the forenoon for provisions and to visit the Harris Tweed depot. Under way at 12.00 to make the passage to Stromness; light variable airs and rain.'

Cape Wrath was weathered (variable weather) in the early hours of the next morning and course set for Hoy Sound, across the approaches to Pentland Firth, and *Blue Jay* reached Stromness in heavy rain. 'Spent the forenoon ashore. Under way at 14.52, the wind being E. strong, and soon there was more rain.'

Having been under way on some twenty-two or twenty-three days, and for most of them in daunting weather, *Blue Jay* had reached her objective and the turning point of the cruise, which was celebrated by a day at anchor in Scapa Bay while the owner 'visited friends at Kirkwall'. And in the morning it was again blowing a gale of wind and rain. She got under way in the afternoon, however, to sail across the Flow and anchor for the night in St. Margaret's, before tackling the crossing of Pentland Firth. Dinwiddy's account of the passage contains valuable pilotage information:

'Having reefed mainsail and mizzen, under way at 04.15, raining and very cold. . . . The wind backed to S.W. by S., course across Pentland Firth was S. 6° W., which meant a long and short (tack) through.

'Duncansby Head was passed at 06.30—$10\frac{1}{2}$ miles to windward in an hour and nine minutes on the *first* of the flood.

'To avoid being carried towards Lowther Rock and to the N. of Muckle Skerry, I had tacked close to Stanger Head and again right to the eddy off Swona Island (which had not fully developed on the early flood) but when N.W. of Muckle Skerry found that the bearing on the lighthouse was hardly changing, and to avoid the risk of being carried on to the Pentland Skerries had to bear away free on the port tack until certain of going clear.'

'This' (commented Dinwiddy mildly), 'and a swirling boil and tumble of tide were the only features of this part of the Pentland.' And the very next sentence is, 'Turned to windward down the east coast, and at 09.53, the weather looking more settled, and the wind being moderate to fresh S.W., shook out reefs'.

The passage of the Caledonian Canal was made under the power of the little engine, which, however, having no reverse gear, was occasionally more than man enough for the job.

When *Blue Jay* was sailing again we have a stirring picture of her in Loch Aber. 'Set all sail and made a fast passage down Loch Aber, the wind N.E., fresh, dead aft. Passed the Narrows against the spring flood, which was boiling strongly through. At 18.30 the wind freshened further, and we lay-to and double-reefed main and mizzen, then continued, goose-winged, down Loch Linnhe and Loch Lynn of Morven.'

For most of the passage home the weather was tempestuous, wind and rain all the way to the chops of the Channel, where, instead, came fog, so dense that Dinwiddy was apprehensive of his landfall. The long paragraph in the log at this point is more than ever a welter of times, courses, bearings, and the rest. But imbedded in it there is an exciting experience; vividly described:

'*July 13*, at 05.10—log 87.5—there was still no wind, and dense fog suddenly came down. Estimated position, Pendeen to the S., distant about 9 miles. At 05.30 heard steamers to S.S.E. blowing fog blasts; altered course S. 10° E., hoping to hear Pendeen fog signal. At 06.10—log 92.4—heard Pendeen ahead; continued on course, and at 06.32 Pendeen appeared by sound about 3 or 4 miles distant; altered course S.W., which would be certain of clearing the Brisons (on which rocks it was reported later a schooner became a total loss that morning) to pick up the Longships fog-gun, and at 06.44 first heard the

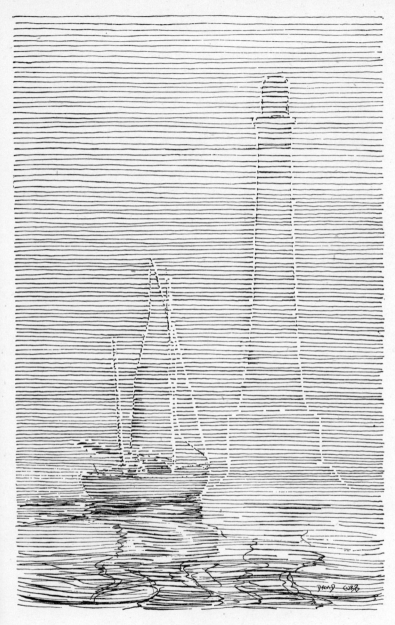

Off the Longships

Longships gun, bearing about S.S.W.; altered course S.W. by S.

'At 07.10 altered course S.S.W., and at 07.36 the gun appearing to be well on the port bow, altered to S. by W.; and its two successive five-minute explosions still appearing to be on the port bow, continued on that course.

'At 07.52 something *suddenly* appeared on the port bow as a weird apparition in the thick fog, and in what seemed only a second assumed its true form of the Longships, and almost at the same moment the gun sounded with a terrific explosion, the lighthouse appearing as a phantom column. And in seconds all was gone again—log 101.'

4 Between the Longships and the Land—'R.C.C.'

MUST not one admire it? After the apparition '——Log 101'!

Dinwiddy later explained that he was keeping an 'inside course' to avoid the steamer traffic that converges at the Longships. That he nearly piled up on that dread spot he thought could only be due to an unindicated, or unwonted, set of the tidal stream.

But when he speaks of an 'inside course' in conjunction with the Longships—how I am reminded! I may have told this yarn before, but, for me, the wonder of it will never be diminished in the telling.

Bound for the Clyde in the ex-12-metre *Noreen* we had left Fowey in the morning, taking the last of the ebb.

One hardly knew what to make of the weather. The glass, moderately high, had been pretty steady, and was steady still. But in the air was a sultry, clammy feel. At any rate, we carried a nice sailing breeze all the way to the Lizard. Here the wind faltered, dwindling away to the faintest of airs from the S.W. During the afternoon and for part of the early evening we contrived to struggle across Mounts Bay.

Towards dark we had the land about Mousehole somewhere on the beam. About now the yacht met a swell rolling in from the S.W., the real long ocean-swell, which emptied the sails of whatever wind they might be holding and made all the canvas slat. This swell might be the forerunner of a blow, and yet there was as yet no more wind. The glass seemed to be holding steady, and the sunset looked not too bad. Nor, perhaps, too good.

But within half an hour it was blowing quite freshly and since we had been longing for such a breeze we let her romp along, just able to steer a nice full-and-by. Ten minutes later we had to take in the big jib, for now there was real weight in the wind.

On this tack it was going to be a ticklish job to weather the Longships, whose light had just been kindled. We fell to watching that light; dead ahead, and now high aloft, and now at our bowsprit's end. But to tack now seemed to promise that the coming night would be spent bucketing about off the Longships in a steeper and steeper sea.

'Ease your mainsheet!'

Now, none of us in *Noreen* had ever before been between the Longships and the land. On the chart, examined by flash-lamp in the gathering dark, the passage looked terrifying. But with eased sheets the old boat was plunging along, and we were now within the Longships warning-sector. A drizzle had started, and it came on thick with mist. At this point the

Longships started its fog-gun, a most eerie and forbidding sound.

The scene during that hour—though it could have lasted nothing like an hour—will for ever remain with me. The great, black, craggy rocks, foam-encircled. The misted high mainland cliffs of Land's End. Another cluster of rocks, black and white. And another lot, and another. And suddenly, dead ahead, an isolated rock, all a-welter. Close aboard to port was the dim grey tower, and high up in it the baleful gleam of its warning sector, and the dull booming of the fog-gun.

And then to look and see, at the thousandth frightened glance, that red light change to white! For we were through, between the Longships and the land!

(To describe the night which followed is beyond my powers, and anyway should not be attempted in this book.)

For his cruise in *Blue Jay*, outlined in the preceding chapter, the Royal Cruising Club awarded Dinwiddy its Claymore Challenge Cup, a trophy, one of three (at that time), to be won for cruises of outstanding merit.

Dinwiddy had become a member of the Royal Cruising Club in that year, 1927. His election meant much to him then, and even more as time went on, when he himself, and his example, came to mean more and more to the club.

The narratives of noteworthy cruises are published each year in the Royal Cruising Club *Journal*, and the awards for each season are based on the respective merits of the cruises therein described. Not that the logs are necessarily submitted with a prize in mind—though that perhaps is a spur to reluctant authorship —for most are sent in out of public spirit, to describe some not-too-much-frequented waters, or to share some pleasurable experience. It follows, then, that they are factual pieces of writing (and this is where one is likely to be unjust to Dinwiddy's gnarled and knotty prose) not concerned with the contributor's thoughts and impressions, but with *facts* and *places*: the navigational difficulties or peculiarities, climate, coinage, depths of water, winds, tides, rise-and-fall, custom regulations, where to anchor or lay alongside, where to shop and what to buy, and in particular, though one might even say in general, what to *avoid*.

This might almost read as suggesting that folk who fly the R.C.C. burgee are a testy, touchy, anti-social lot of fellows. Well, there is no denying that some of them are. For yacht cruising would seem to have this in common with the process of growing old: that one's more eccentric characteristics become exaggerated.

Although, by the way, the *Journal* is circulated only to members of the club, in more recent years some copies have been available to the public. And if one may testify as a member of that public I should say that, on the whole, the matter published is first-class. Its pages have been the first to print some of the most notable of all amateur seafaring achievements—the accounts of Macpherson's prolonged ocean-voyaging, to name only one—and so in course of time the possessor of these volumes has formed a small, but in a sense, select yachting library.

Small and select—the cliché popped out. For the fact is that, while it is not small, the Royal Cruising Club is a select body. Though while one has no means of knowing whether it has ever of intention sought to be exclusive—at least in the determined manner of clubs whose very *raison d'être* appears to be exclusiveness—there the fact is, you cannot select unless you exclude. But rather would one suggest that whatever proportion the club may have of these two qualities, results from the club's policy, which, while unexpressed (so far as one knows), is that it encourages the true spirit of sea-adventuring no more strongly than it discourages all that may appear even to savour of the self-advertising stunt.

Hence, doubtless, the extreme and often absurd degree to which its members, at any rate in their written narratives, carry the famous—or notorious, for some nations hate it—English cult of the understatement.

When Dinwiddy became a member of the club its commodore was still the venerable Sir Arthur Underhill, who was its founder in 1880, and who has left us this note on its origin.

'Some time before the autumn of 1879 I had been surprised to find that although there were upwards of fifty yacht clubs in the United Kingdom, they were all devoted to racing and not one to cruising, by which I mean the pastime of visiting places in this country and abroad in one's own yacht carrying one's habitation on one's back like a snail, and enjoying the change of harbour from time to time without the trouble of packing and hiring accommodation at each place visited. There was also the great pleasure of learning and practising the art of navigation, and the combat of the opposing forces of wind and water (as interesting a game as one could wish for), with just that amount of danger and hard knocks to make it a sport as well as a pastime.

'Accordingly in 1880 I got together a few friends with similar tastes . . .'

This may read somewhat quaintly today, when on every sizeable water thousands practise what this man preached. But all the same is not one reminded of that saying of Emerson's: 'An institution is the lengthened shadow of a man?'

5 'The High Attempting Spirit'

DINWIDDY had his permanent moorings at Galmpton, or more exactly, a cable or so away, at Greenway. Those familiar with the River Dart will know this to be on the Kingswear or eastern side of the river, something more than a mile above the railway station and 'just round the bend', where the hills diminish somewhat and the river (though not the channel) widens. It is one of the sweetest spots in all the world.

One of them. For there is an air, as much as there is a look about all yacht anchorages, which make them, to folk of our kind, the most captivating of scenes.

And folded and tucked away in every coastline, scooped out of the islands and atolls in every sea, are enchanting little anchorages past the counting and which the longest life would not have span enough to find. But this thought is quite bearable, because God, Who allots that span, has provided each of us with his special favourite, chosen haven. For Dinwiddy this was Greenway.

In its miniature way this spot possesses, and combines, all the advantages that the sailing directions praise—when they can find them!—namely, sufficient depth of water, firm and clean holding-ground, shelter from the prevailing wind at least, and facilities not too distant on shore for provisioning and watering. But to fare farther is not always to fare worse, and small craft look for something more. Quiet, for one thing; absence of motion as much as absence of noise.

Another indispensable (as I think it) is that green things shall lie close about; as at my beloved Benodet, where the pines stand slimly at the water's very edge; as at remote Oyster Bay (though there *is* a great clubhouse rising among those pearly marshes); as in the water-pit of Lulworth, perilous in steep places; and as in my secret——, where the meadows and sedges are coloured with unusual flowers; as in the sanctuary of Beaulieu River; as at Itchenor and Boshom, beyond which the downs rise 'so noble and so bare'; as in Sou' Deep, Poole, and at Helford, and at Tresco, and at—you know where.

I used to think, too, that there was something fine in having a lighthouse near: one seems to lie the more snugly with the knowledge that close at hand is a danger grave enough to warrant that permanent giant sentinel with its reassuring sweep of beam or placid and steadfast single eye; but, oh, with so agonized a cry! Even now I can, as it were, cut out hearing so as to leave only the dolorous hooting wail of Execution Light—well-named indeed!—always to me the characteristic voice of Long Island Sound. But then what of our own Bishops, in the Scillies, whose desolate sobs used to appal me when in the old *Czarina*, lying off Tresco. Outside Hell, was there ever such lost wailing?

34

All are delightful. Which is the dearest? So by an almost inevitable train of thought we are back in the Dart.

You would think this place and this river could content a man for ever; or, at the very least, would be sorrowfully hard to leave. How, then, does it come about that the men of Devon have been our most far-sailing seamen?

Listen to what is told us in an old book: 'To instance one among many, Humphrey Gilbert was of a high attempting spirit, a skilful mathematician and hydrographer, though not equally favoured of fortune. Yet may the great volume of his virtue be read whose project be to discover the remote countries of America . . .'

Where do you think this lofty soul was born and had his home? Greenway.

You can see the house still, a small mansion house standing among gardens by the riverside. (It was standing empty when I was last there, by the way, but soon afterwards became the home of a prolific and popular writer of thrillers.)

Humphrey's widowed mother became the wife of Walter Ralegh, 'Whose son' (to quote again the old chronicler), 'the renowned Sir Walter Ralegh thus became Humphrey Gilbert's half-brother. This progeny hath long flourished in these parts and God grant still it may'.

Since, as boys together, Humphrey and Walter rowed and sailed and swam and fished in the Dart, the progeny of the great Devonians hath indeed flourished in these parts. We old chaps think of Dartside as a place to settle when we can go to sea no more.

But it is mainly a nursery. Look at that great college on the hill!

Leaving Greenway on June 20, 1929, with Eales Bartlett as shipmate, 'the high attempting spirit' with whose voyaging these pages are mainly concerned set out in *Blue Jay* to circumnavigate Ireland. This was accomplished in the space of five weeks, logging just on 1,500 miles.

Thus, in duration as well as in distance, the Irish cruise resembled the Orkney cruise, an average of 300 miles sailed weekly—which is a *tempo*, so to speak which perhaps would be too *troppo* for most of us. On the whole, however, *Blue Jay* had good weather and fair winds for the Irish cruise, and it is perhaps for this reason that Dinwiddy's log records so many agreeable days, or hours, or moments, that the reader, also, may find it agreeable if we attempt a précis.

On the first night out, the wind blowing up stiffly from N.N.W., *Blue Jay* brought up off Cawsand (western shore of Plymouth Sound, and a quiet anchorage with the wind from this quarter, as the Camaret crabbers well know). The next day's sail brought them to the Scillies, when 'opportunity was taken to explore St. Agnes Island and to visit again the sub-tropical garden at Tresco.

'Of the many yachts that sail west as far as Falmouth and Helford, it always surprises me that so few make the short passage to these delightful islands with their choice of safe anchorages. As is my invariable custom when in port, I dined ashore at St. Mary's, and afterwards we sailed through Broad and North Sounds and round the western dangers, the rocks looking formidable under a breaking swell and in a failing light.'

After a day and a night at sea the Knockmillie-down mountains were sighted at dawn, distant many miles, the day breaking fine. A bearing of Ballycotton was got by breakfast-time, and the yacht anchored in Queenstown in the early evening; distance made good, 151 miles.

The cruise round Ireland was to be made west-about and *Blue Jay* sailed for Baltimore. 'Between Toe Head and Stack rocks the wind had freshened and was dead aft; the sea was rather rough and we were sailing at a great pace, but the big schooner *Magdalene* had come up from astern and left us standing.'

May I break in here with a reminiscence of *Magdalene*? This superb schooner was built in the United States (in 1913) but her designer was an Irishman, J. Beavor Webb, a man of genius. Oddly, he was born near the Old Head of Kinsale, that is to say, in the vicinity where Dinwiddy saw his wonderful creation. During the good while I have known her she was owned by Mr. W. Jameson. Reference to *Lloyd's Register of Yachts* shows her present name to be *Kirin* and her owner a retired naval officer.

Dinwiddy, however, was much less interested in *Magdalene* than in a vessel he was told of that very afternoon when *Blue Jay* brought up off Baltimore. 'Ashore I was shown where *Saoirse* was built; and the pride of Baltimore was evident in being the starting and ending place of her world cruise.' (The reference is, of course, to Conor O'Brien's famous world-circumnavigation, 1923–5, during which period *Saoirse* sailed 31,000 miles in 280 sailing days.)

Blue Jay's next port was Bantry, from where she sailed over to Glengariff. Dinwiddy was ecstatic. 'The most fairy harbour that I ever sailed into; blue water dotted with islands, rocky and rugged, but with luxuriant Irish green vegetation contrasting with the dark green of fir trees, and the rugged mountains, blue in the easterly haze, forming a background.'

As though all after Glengariff must appear anti-climatic, the log contains little but pilotage-notes for the next few pages, until Killary Bay was reached, when we have this entry.

'*July 8.* Made the entrance to Killary Bay at 15.45, and anchored at its head in $1\frac{1}{4}$ fathoms at 17.16. Ashore I heard of a yacht that had anchored here some weeks previously, but was not able to find her name, and her identity remained obscure until after my return home'—when he learned that the visitor had been none other than A. G. H. Macpherson.

At this point in the cruise continuous rain fell for 60 hours!

Despite this *Blue Jay* got under way for Donegal, on the passage thither rounding Achill Head, which was passed, a mile off, at midnight, though there was light enough in the sky to reveal its mass, which towers 2,182 ft. The following night she was off Donegal,

'*Magdalene*' *overtakes* '*Blue Jay*'

where, after some careful sounding in the dark, for the banks were covered, she eventually found an anchorage about two miles below the town. Here she remained a day watering and provisioning, 'and I explored Donegal, Ballyshannon on the fine river Erne, and Bundoran, and pulled down from Donegal in the boat in the evening.'

Bound next for Lough Swilly, Bloody Foreland was rounded against a foul tide but with a strong commanding breeze, S.E. by S. In Lough Swilly she brought up off Portsalon, to find in the morning, the wind having gone S.E., in fierce squalls, that this had become a dangerous lee shore. She successfully clawed off, under close reefs, however, and later the owner was able to console and refresh himself with 'a very excellent dinner ashore at Rathmullan in the small Pier Hotel'.

Thereafter, for the remainder of the cruise, the weather remained broken.

Being now homeward-bound, and lying at Larne, Dinwiddy fell ill. The log breathes no hint of it, and the information comes from Bartlett, who says that it was the only time he had seen his owner so much as out of sorts. Apparently a doctor at Larne had told him he should rest; but Dinwiddy was longing for home, as sick people so often do, and *Blue Jay* put to sea on a rainy day, wind S.W., intending to make for Milford Haven.

When only a short way on her course, however, the wind chopped round to N.N.E., with heavy rain, and, the southerly swell persisting, there was soon a most uncomfortable sea.

Bartlett was at the tiller, Dinwiddy in his bunk

below, where he noted in the log: 'Throughout the whole day the rain and the uneasy sea continued, with not enough following wind to keep the sails asleep. Everything above deck rattling, chafing, banging and crashing on the uneven swell; down below the noise above sounded like hell let loose, and the whole air is rain-soaked.' About his own condition not a word.

In the circumstances course was altered for Fishguard; and the yacht was easier now that the breeze was brought more on her quarter. Approaching Fishguard there was another shift of wind and *Blue Jay* had to beat into port. Bartlett's spell at the helm had lasted 36 hours.

They were under way early next morning, all the same, Bartlett standing another long watch. Indeed, he more or less took the yacht home single-handed; Dinwiddy never becoming fit enough to stay at the tiller longer than the relief for meals.

All ended well, and Dinwiddy was much more himself when they came to moorings at Greenway after sunset on July 22. Total distance made good, 1,497 miles.

In a paragraph summarizing the cruise, after a tribute to the courtesy and hospitality everywhere met with, Dinwiddy comments, as so many have done, on the neglect of the west coast of Ireland by yachtsmen. 'We had these waters practically to ourselves; after leaving Scilly and until again within the approaches to Falmouth . . . only three yachts were seen. And the only other vessels sighted were a few English and Scottish steam trawlers, a few local fishing craft off Valentia and Galway, two or three coasting steamers, and some ubiquitous Frenchmen of characteristic type, tending their pots and sailing among the rocks with the same confidence that they show off their own west coast.'

For this cruise the Claymore Cup was again awarded to Dinwiddy, the judge being Claud Worth.

PART TWO
'Eternal Wave'

6 'Eternal Wave'

WINNING the Claymore Cup twice, for successive cruises, had the odd result of turning Dinwiddy's enthusiasm and energies to motor-boating.

'With years accumulating, on long passages shorthanded the shelter of a wheelhouse would be a comfort and an advantage over the strain of the long hours in an open cockpit; and the working of the ship, with the watching and care of the engine-room, would leave few idle moments.'

These are his own words. And it is true that at this time, 1930, he was in his middle fifties. But that the convenience and comfort of a wheelhouse and so on was not his only motive is suggested, I think, in another sentence where he speaks of a motor yacht being, 'Something different, while retaining the same interests of navigation and seafaring, and of visiting countries and places in the most interesting way.'

I myself have come to the opinion, reading between the lines of his log-books and letters, that he had an underlying purpose, and that this was the desire to demonstrate 'in his generation' that motor-boating or motor-yachting was not a slighter, nor indeed separate thing, but that it *could be* as worthwhile, as adventurous and as rewarding as cruising under sail.

For that was his achievement. And while he was achieving it he was writing a new chapter in yachting history.

He was from the start decided on his choice of craft. 'As to type, the obsolescent 43-ft. Watson lifeboat seemed to be *the boat*, with the added joy of putting her in service again.' And he could have added another joy, that of doing the work of conversion with that enviable skill of his.

Among the R.N.L.I. lifeboats available just then for disposal was the *James Stevens*. A Watson 43-ft. pulling-sailing type, this boat had been built by the Thames Ironworks, a firm renowned for the excellence of its workmanship. The *James Stevens* was first commissioned at Queenstown in 1901; but before long her station became Fenit, County Cork, where she remained in service, not uneventfully, from 1902 to 1928, after which, time-expired, she was sold out of the service to Dinwiddy, whose successful bid was the nowadays inconsiderable sum of £70.

Converting the *James Stevens* into a motor yacht occupied Dinwiddy for a couple of winters. At some time during the task he arranged for her name to be changed—No! Let us keep the word—to be converted to *Eternal Wave*. For surely it was an inspiration.

How often have I wondered just how Dinwiddy came to hit on it. But I must have expressed this curiosity long ago, possibly at the time, for in one of his letters I have come across the following:

'What did recall to me my thoughts in naming *Eternal Wave* was a phrase about waves in Hilaire Belloc's *Hills and the Sea*, "Steep, curling, unintermittently, rank upon rank upon rank", and how much more so does the small power-yacht take every one, instead of riding them as in sail.'

In the meantime, believing so fine a phrase must be a quotation, I had asked Mr. J. B. Atkins, so erudite in all such matters, where it could have come from. He, however, doubted whether 'it could have come from anywhere. Tennyson wrote of "the wave that went round the world", which is getting on that way.' J.B.A. then added what he called 'the flippant suggestion' that it may have been a contraction of the first two lines of the famous hymn for those at sea:

> *Eternal Father, strong to save,*
> *Whose arm doth bind the restless wave.*

Perhaps it is nigh-on blasphemous that this in turn should recall to one the last two lines from the *Ballad of the Bolivar*:

> *Euchred God Almighty's storm,*
> *Bluffed the Eternal sea.*

Lines which surely no seaman would utter for fear of being struck dead!

However, J.B.A. rightly went on to point out that the juxtaposition of 'eternal' with 'wave' is far from logical. But I do not think that so important, as that, when you come to think of it, the association of those two words possesses a meaning of the most poignant kind.

For do not they associate the fleeting generations of men with that part of creation that fadeth not away? Recall Byron:

> *Dark-heaving—boundless, endless, and sublime,*
> *The image of eternity.*

When I was in church the Sunday after writing this, Parson gave out 'Hymn 168—Ancient and Modern'. And perhaps you will guess how it delighted me to find:

> *One name . . .*
> *The everlasting sea proclaims,*
> *Echoing Angelic songs.*

What are the wild waves saying? *Echoing Angelic songs!*

7 *Maiden Voyage*

ALTHOUGH no type is more distinctive, and none is more familiar, a fact or two about *Eternal Wave* ought perhaps to be given here.

Her length is 43 ft., the beam 12·5 ft. She draws 3·5 ft. of water. The main member in the construction is the keel, cast-iron, 13 in. broad and in depth only a couple of inches less, which runs plumb from the stem almost to the bows. Extra ballast, three-quarters of a ton of lead, is stowed aft.

'Her hull, with the characteristic turtle-back decks at bow and stern, and the bold surrounding cork fender, also the stanchions and lifelines, were unaltered and the side-decks with their carlines, were also retained', wrote Dinwiddy at the time of the conversion.

'But the main deck and the rowing-thwarts were removed to make way for the accommodation. This consists—under a cambered coachroof with tumble-home coamings—of a foc'sle with fixed bunk, engine-room, wheelhouse with chart-table, galley to one side and lavatory on the other, then the saloon, and, aft of all, a double cabin; all having full headroom. Under the side-decks, where there are also large lockers and stowage for warps, are the main fuel tanks.'

The main engine, from which a speed of 7 knots could be relied on, was a 30 h.p. Kelvin-Ricardo, installed to port. As an auxiliary and stand-by in case of breakdown, a 15 h.p. motor was installed to star-board. The fuel used was kerosene, of which 200 gallons were carried, sufficient for a cruising-radius of 650 miles. The water tanks held 87 gallons.

Dinwiddy had remarked that he chose an R.N.L.I. lifeboat for the reason—sole, simple, and sufficient—that she was 'the most seaworthy type of small craft'.

This he duly proceeded to demonstrate, so soon as the boat was ready, by making for Alderney Race, in conditions when that locality would be quite the last place where most of us would chose to be: the ebb-tide running, at full Springs, with a W'ly wind strong to gale.

'Much water came aboard, but she stood the test well.'

He had to admit, however, that she had the defect of her great virtue, and that the wonderful degree of buoyancy characteristic of an R.N.L.I. lifeboat made the boat so lively as to be most fatiguing in a seaway. 'But with a sturdy heavy motion that gives confidence in her seaworthiness.'

But Bartlett thought she behaved like a brute in such conditions, and he made no bones about it.

'She was the most uncomfortable ship I ever sailed in. Steaming head-on to a fresh breeze she would exhaust anyone. Her best point of sailing was running, and provided you did not let her broach-to, you could keep her running in almost a gale of wind.'

It was also Bartlett's opinion that Dinwiddy would have done better to retain the centre-plate and have had means of setting some sail, which the boat had originally.

'You couldn't expect her to behave the same. It was all right in good weather, but when the boat was being punished in the way I described it was like hell let loose—rolling and pitching, and making a passage very tiring.'

Eternal Wave was commissioned for her maiden voyage in the spring of 1931. Dinwiddy and Bartlett formed the ship's company. Destination—Oslo, in Norway; by way of the Zuider Zee and the Kiel Canal.

She left the River Dart at the beginning of June and returned thereto on July 7—again five weeks!— having accomplished the cruise as planned. Much bad weather was met with, and a large proportion of the head-winds so roundly cursed by Bartlett.

But, regrettably, as we must think, in his acute concern to make light of this achievement—which, in 1931, had only one possible parallel—there is no denying that Dinwiddy also succeeded in making his narrative dull. But since this is only my own view (induced perhaps by over-familiarity, for I have read the log not less than three times and have also copied it out in full), it would be presumptuous to attempt to summarize it without giving a few direct quotations.

First, then, the passage from Dover:

'We left the Granville Dock at 02.55 on Thursday, June 4th, a fine night but hazy. Outside course was set 120°, with the flood stream wide on the quarter, for Outer Ruytingen Buoy, and then Dyck L.V., which was made at 17.19. We then proceeded by the inner channel past Dunkerque, and northerly by the Zuidecote Pass and through West Deep (all reminiscent of these waters in 1916). Visibility was only about two miles, and a fresh north north east wind made a short and wet head sea. The historical Zeebrugge mole was rounded at 15.08, and after looking for a billet we made fast between dolphins in the fishing harbour, where there is perfect shelter, space, and a good depth of water. Distance 79 miles. A large fishing fleet lay in tiers alongside the quays. Ashore I saw the impressive Belgian St. George's Day Memorial and the scene of all it commemorates in an otherwise uninteresting place.

'Under way the following day at 04.20 and rounding the mole, course was set 16°. The wind was north east strong, and against the ebb from the Schelde over the shallows the sea was short and rough. After proceeding about 6 miles the engine was running hot, so we turned 16 points and ran under the starboard engine.

'Back in Zeebrugge Harbour the water circulation in the main engine was investigated and eventually put right, and we were under way again at 10.15. We proceeded on the 16° course, then north easterly for about 50 miles, literally through the shallows off the mouths of the Schelde and Maas, the strong head wind causing a very short rough sea all day, into which

'Eternal Wave' off the Schelde

Eternal Wave plunged in a continuous deluge of water, making navigation difficult with obscured visibility and a swinging compass. At 00.30 on June 5th we made Ymuiden Harbour, and anchored. Distance run 101 miles.

'At 07.50 we locked into the Amsterdam Ship Canal. The barometer had dropped 0·25 in the past 36 hours to 29·80, and it was raining with a fresh easterly wind . . .'

The approaches to Oslo:

'We were under way again at 02.38, the barometer 29·54, the wind very strong south west by south. Clear of the shelter of the islands it was blowing very hard to a gale. *Eternal Wave* was plunging into a rough sea, and the swinging compass and a continuous deluge of water made picking up navigational marks difficult.

'At 03.10 the engine was running hot, doubtless due to an air lock in the water circulation, as *Eternal Wave* jumped her keel out of the water in the rough sea. So we put about and returned to Selandertorp under the starboard engine. It continued to blow a gale all day. . . . In the afternoon I walked to Stromstadt, a small, old world town only two miles distant, but round an inlet of the sea, and by very devious and hilly tracks, the country covered by hillocks of worn granite boulders with Irish green undergrowth; it took well over an hour's hard walking. By the evening the glass had commenced to rise, but the wind, which had veered two points, was still very strong.

'On Friday, June 19th, the wind had eased a little but was still strong west south west; the barometer still low at 29·65. We were under way at 08.25 and found a still rough sea outside which deluged over the bow, but we made the Skreia Buoy to the north westward, and proceeded northerly, open to the full run from the North Sea, but occasionally gaining a little shelter from the outlying islands. It was a fine day, the wind backing to south west continued strong, but as we got into the mouth of the wide Oslo Fjord the sea lessened, and at 12.00 we passed under the lee of Rano Island, and from there had an easier passage. At 15.35 we passed Kaholm Lighthouse on the narrows near Drobak, and rounding the north end of the Nosodden Peninsula at 17.15 proceeded between the islands to the northeastward, and found a billet near the centre of the city in the Piperviken, Oslo, at 18.14. Barometer 29·70.

Here, fifteen days out from Dover, 1,168 miles on the log, *Eternal Wave* was at her port of destination.

We should get no change if we asked what were Dinwiddy's feelings. Nor was he communicative of his impressions of Norway and the Norwegians, and their capital city.

'We remained at Oslo the following day, which was very sunny, doing some adjustments in the engine-room, getting provisions and some Danish charts of the Little Belt, and Bartlett varnished the deckwork, which had become badly in need. I saw something of Oslo, a very fine city most beautifully situated. *Eternal Wave* appeared to evoke interest as something unusual to the Norwegians, and I had pressing invitations to lie at the Yacht Club, but as the Yacht Club was on a part of the Fjord remote from the city, and time was short, I remained in the Piperviken. H.M.S. *Repulse* and *Renown* anchored in the roadstead in the forenoon.'

'On Sunday, June 21st, we were under way at 05.31, a fine morning, calm, and the barometer rather low, but steady at 29·68. We proceeded down the Fjord . . .' Homeward bound.

The weather continued bad, awful most of it, and the words 'blew very hard', 'still blowing strong', 'wind strong to gale' recur in the log with depressing monotony.

Eternal Wave's homeward voyage was down the east coast of Jutland, through the Kiel Canal, then to Lowestoft, Dover, Cowes. Though the log is still intricately packed with pilotage details, valuable to cruisers in the same waters, the 'general reader' would most likely own to finding it fairly stiff going—like *Eternal Wave* herself—though here and there are entries which do convey a feeling of a scene.

'At 11.20 off the south end of Basto Island the wind and sea had increased. I had intended making Langesund on the Norwegian south east coast . . . but with the heavy sea it would be a bad passage off a lee shore, and pilotage difficult under the conditions. I therefore decided to find an anchorage and altered course for Eloen Island. The wind continued to increase, and at 13.05 we made a perfect little natural harbour between Engelsviko Island and the Norwegian mainland, and anchored. But there was one defect, for during the afternoon the anchor dragged—my first experience of ground-tackle not holding—it was found to be a weedy bottom on soft mud, and we made fast to a mooring dolphin. Such dolphins are frequent on these coasts, and consist of a number of stakes driven into the bottom, drawn and lashed together at the top. It continued to blow very hard, though by evening the barometer had only fallen to 29·61.'

End of the cruise: 'We remained at Dover for a few days making good varnish and paintwork, and going outside to the basin to scrub and recoat. The weed, in spite of proper anti-fouling coating, had grown so badly since launching in May that it required sharp steel scrapers and two tides to do the work. Under way at 03.55, proceeded down channel, making Cowes against the invariable south west wind and rather rough sea. We then made Swanage against a strong wind, which eased somewhat in the evening, and allowed a still wet passage to Portland by midnight, and starting at 04.35 were back in the River Dart at 12.10 on the following day.'

The total distance made good was 2,224 miles.

The cruises made under the burgee of the Royal Cruising Club that year were judged by no less a personage than Claud Worth ('. . . of the straightest sect', etc.), who, making his awards, said:

'By the rules the judge is required to take into account enterprise in exploring coasts and harbours, seamanship, navigation and pilotage, and distance made good and number of ports visited having regard to the capabilities of the vessel and the time available. I consider *Driac's* cruise to be the best (Portsmouth to Malta), closely approached by that of *Emanuel* (Biscay). Of the other cruises those of *Escape* (Norway) and *Frolic* (round Ireland) are of nearly equal merit, with *Eternal Wave's* cruise a good third.'

Claud Worth then set out the reasons why he accorded the cruises their respective positions. And it must be admitted that he did so in a manner so authoritative, and indeed so Olympian, that others can only mutely concur.

When it comes to Dinwiddy's turn he shows a school-masterly severity:

'At some date not mentioned *Eternal Wave* motored from Dartmouth to Dover. Proceeded north . . . Thence she motored along the coast to Oslo. . . . Afterwards *Eternal Wave* got under way for Dartmouth, but for this again no dates are given.'

Is it not clear that besides the *timelessness* of the trip, so to speak, there was something else and something bigger that was somehow distasteful to Worth— namely, this 'motoring' and all this 'proceeding'? It is clear, it seems to me, because at the end of his analysis Worth adds, 'A good cruise carried out as one would expect of a man who has twice won the Claymore Cup *in sail*' (my italics).

8 Thomas Fleming Day

TWENTY years ago a 2,000-odd mile voyage by motor-boat was a far rarer thing than it has since become. But it was not unique. The unique thing had been achieved twenty years before *Eternal Wave*, nineteen years to be correct, when, in 1912, the *Detroit* crossed the Atlantic.

Years before that, the feasibility of such an undertaking had been proclaimed by the American Magazine *The Rudder*. Eventually it was achieved by the editor himself, Thomas Fleming Day.

The *Detroit* was 35 ft. in length, equipped with a 16 h.p. Scripps engine. On the passage from Sandy Hook to Queenstown the vessel carried a thousand gallons of petrol, of which she consumed about fifty gallons a day. The trip turned out to be a nightmare. For some description of it, and of the *Detroit's* subsequent history, we can fortunately refer to a letter from a reader of *The Motor Boat*, published in that journal a good while back:

Sir,
Referring to the *Detroit* in which the late Thos. F. Day made a trip from Detroit to St. Petersburg (now Leningrad), I can explain what happened to her. Day did not cross the

Atlantic alone; he had three amateurs with him and one paid hand. They had stormy weather all the way across the Atlantic, and when they arrived in Ireland they had to be carried to the clubhouse, for they could not stand upon steady ground. They had one or two fires on board while crossing, and they also had some trouble with their ballast, which was in lead shot and which, during the rolling of the boat, had worked its way to one side and resulted in an unpleasant list.

I went on board at St. Petersburg and found that they had bored a circle of holes with a brace in the bulkhead between the engine-room aft and the central well of the boat, which contained five or six long steel fuel cylinders and the shot ballast. Through this hole they somehow managed to dig over some of the shot to the other side. That central well took up about half the length of the boat, leaving them only a small cabin forward with two bunks. They used these bunks in turn.

Stormy weather followed them right up to St. Petersburg. The boat was left at the River Yacht Club at Krestoffsky Island, St. Petersburg. I was a member of that club, and I remember Mr. Day saying that he wouldn't do the trip again if he were offered a million dollars—and I don't wonder. There were too many on board to make the journey comfortable.

The boat was lying there some time and was eventually sold to some monastery in the interior of Russia.

Yours faithfully,
H. P. E. SANDERS.

Westcliff-on-Sea.

If in truth 'the style is the man', then Day must have possessed a lovable character. I think of him as a sort of Dinwiddy, but poetical, super-charged, and Americanized!

Thomas Fleming Day founded *The Rudder* in 1890, and was its editor for twenty-six years. The Old Man, as he came to be called, printed in the first issue of his own column, *Round the Clubhouse Fire*, a set of precepts which he practised as well as preached. 'While I hold my place at this fireside but one spirit shall animate its discourses—a desire to keep honest, just and clean, our sport. To keep it what it has always been—a manly pastime. To inspire in those who engage in it a love of fair play and an ambition to be sportsmen without strain or reproach.'

The Old Man often used to begin his column with a remark something in the tone of this specimen: 'I have not much time and less space to waste on you people this month . . . but I will condescend to discuss a few favourite topics'. And off he would go for a page or so of forthright good stuff. One month (February, 1902) he launched out as follows: 'Can a motor launch be built and engined to cross the Western Ocean from Sandy Hook to Queenstown? I say, "Yes".'

He would! But, as we have seen, the execution of the object had to be deferred for ten years.

Not less than Dinwiddy, Day was a courageous sailor of small craft long before the *Detroit* adventure. His greatest exploit was the voyage, in 1901, from Providence, R.I., to Rome. His boat was the 25-ft. *Sea Bird*, which was of the hard-chine type, for which the Old Man had, or professed to have, a fondness. With the reader's leave I would like to quote a couple of paragraphs from his narrative, for its own sake, and for its manifestation of what we might almost begin to call the Eternal Wave spirit. To begin with he describes a shake-down trip in *Sea Bird*, some hundreds of miles offshore:

'I decided to heave-to, as it was still thick and breezy and we were well to the south of our latitude. The fog was blowing over in huge chunks, and it made things look nasty and feel worse. We were well in the edge of the Gulf Stream, the water being eighty degrees and full of Gulf weed. When the sun rose it was a deep beautiful blue (the water, not the sun). I rolled up the jib and stopped it to the stay, took in the mizzen, gave her a bit of mainsheet, and all was ready for a comfortable drift. But before going down into warmer quarters I stood for some minutes in the companion watching *Sea Bird* ride the seas.

'It was a sight to gladden your heart. She took the big ones as lightly and gracefully as the creature after whom she is named. Not a drop of water except a light spray touched her decks, and she neither pounded forward nor slapped aft. I could not help contrasting her actions with those of a modern up-to-date boat under similar conditions. Imagine one of your long, full over-hang traps hove-to in such water. What a banging and fussing! One thing that helped the *Sea Bird* was having the ballast inside the boat and evenly distributed over the bottom, not heaped in one chunk directly under the keel. The consequence of this is that she rises bodily, her whole length lifting on the wave almost at the same moment, instead of rising bow and then stern, as outside-weight boats do.

'Now that I have shown you the way, I hope that many will follow the *Sea Bird's* track. It will do you good, and after the venture is safely made you will have more confidence in yourself as a sailor and in your yacht as a sea craft.'

But there; that will almost do. Though we should be ingrates not to remind ourselves that among much stirring verse Thomas Day was the author of the lines beginning:

> *I sing the Sailor of the Sail, breed of the oaken heart,*
> *Who drew the world together and spread our race apart.*

And ending:

> *Unsung, unrung, forgotten, sleeps the Sailor of the Sail.*

Day himself died in 1927, his ashes being scattered in the sea off New York.

9 Screw and Sail

AT the very beginning of all his writings about *Eternal Wave* her owner put this sentence:

'Quite shamelessly *Eternal Wave* is a small motor yacht.'

Are not all of us constantly using some such expression, to convey a meaning opposite to what the words say? 'I apologize for it, but there; my boat is a motorboat.'

For even so late as the early thirties of this present century, when the use of the auxiliary engine was already well-nigh universal, the convention still persisted, that while on land the motor was respected—and indeed had long become a manifestation of respectability!—there was something smacking of vulgarity in its use on water. Above all by the kind of man who had twice won the Claymore Cup 'in sail'!

Possibly it is true that seafarers cling longer to conservative thoughts and ways. How scornful were the men of the clipper-ship era of the new-fangled steamers! 'Giving up the sea, and going in for steam', was one expression of it. Again, how recent it was, as these things go, that the Royal Navy accorded its engineering branch equal status with the executive.

And running through it all one can identify a thread of snobbery, of the special English kind. That patronage which became the established hand-out—though one could say 'hand-off'—of the parvenu. But in the second generation, to whom the upstart has bequeathed a pile of money, the tune is changed. And in another generation—why! Need one go on?

The supreme service of the engine to yachting, as I see it, is that it makes easier the amateur's path down to the sea. The point needs no emphasis. A beginner buys a motor-boat 'off the peg', not yet troubled with, because he does not know about, the multitudinous requirements and the beloved intricacies of sail-and-spar. Now and immediately he can push off from the shore, a marine motorist—abhorrent phrase!

Mark now what happens. One really fine day he fancies he would like a bit of sail 'just to steady her' or 'in case of engine failure', as he explains it to himself. But the true reason is that, unconscious of it, he has been taken gently into custody by the winds. Thrillingly he feels the canvas fill and draw, the boat lists, the clangour of machinery ceases—*she is sailing*!

And so henceforth, unless he be the man in more than a thousand insensible to a joy of motion such as is matched for its freedom only perhaps by the flight of birds—henceforth he is a sailor first and a motorist second: and though there is no *earthly* reason why he should abandon his engine, he will in a very real sense submit himself to the authority of the *heavens*.

The immense improvement in reliability and all-round efficiency of the modern marine motor is, in a general way, one of the best developments in yacht-cruising. Even the auxiliary steam engines, more pliable and obedient than the earlier petrol or other motors, used to give more trouble than they were worth; though to say as much may reveal a personal prejudice resulting from our experiences in the dear old *Czarina* . . .

To apply the power in that noble schooner of ours, two hands from the watch used to lumber aft with a gigantic key which was used, when inserted in its orifice, to put the screw into action. Then we had to stow the sails and hoist the funnel, which was a telescopic one, half sliding down inside the other half, by means of a tackle from the triatic stay.

And (answer, old shipmates!) how frequently on a day of fickle airs had we to totter aft with that key, stow the sail, hoist the funnel—or reverse these evolutions! Up funnel—down sails! Up sails—down funnel!

You can put it shortly by saying that in that ship the machinery was used, not abused. To a sailor, is there any sight more irritating, nay, distressing, than a graceful craft smokily *chug-chugging* along in a smart breeze with her canvas stowed under the sail-covers and the mainboom in its crutch? This you can see in any port on any summer day. And at Cowes, in Cowes week, even! As when some smart modern racing craft, the moment she crosses the finishing-line, drops all her canvas no-how and starts—puff-puff—motoring to her moorings.

(One sometimes thinks of what the professor said

66

about kissing, which he called 'osculation': 'The excuse should be adequate and the occasion infrequent.')

On the other hand, in our old schooner (and I promise not to mention her any more), the old man delighted in the evolution known as the running-moor. Sailing along with full way on—but the precise spot where she was to be brought up already in the skipper's eye—presently, at the exact instant, he would roar 'Let go!' Down would splash the left bower anchor, out rumble the cable—out and out to 100 fathoms or to its bitter end. Then again 'Let go!' Splash goes the right bower. Now, haul in on the port cable and slack away on the starboard, until they are 'middled', and the ship rides to equal scope on each. *Beautiful!*

But there, this is a subject which too readily tends to the solemnity which chills much good yachting talk. May I therefore spin an old yarn, probably fresh to this generation, for so far as I know it has not been seen in print since forty or more years ago, when it appeared in one of the very early numbers of the *Yachting Monthly*.

'I was telling you about the *Queen of the West*', said the narrator. 'By jove, we had a devil of a time in that vessel. I was only a *Chokra*, so I remember it all. We lay in 'Frisco for weeks and weeks waiting for a crew. We got one at last, but by gad they were a pretty lot of beauties. I'm damned if one of them knew the jib-boom from the binnacle. And somehow we could not teach them anything. It turned out that they were a lot of shanghaied tailors, not seamen at all.

'Steer! Why, I steered that ship myself for three days on end. Never left the wheel. Never? Well, hardly ever. You see, old chap, when we put the ship about we missed stays every time.

'What was to be done? Suddenly an idea flashed on me and I put it into execution at once.

'These things in trousers, though knowing nothing of a sailorman's job, were all first-class hands at Monte. Now I said to myself, "We shall see what we shall see."

'On every rope, on every sheet and stay, I put a card.

'Now when the dear old Skipper shouted, "Helm's a-lee, raise tacks and sheets!" nothing happened. But when I took command and bellowed, "Now my bully boys, Ante up! Stand by your King! Let go your Queen! Spades haul!" Well, things began to move a bit.

'And will you believe me when I tell you that inside a fortnight I worked that crew up to such a pitch of efficiency that when the Old Man decided to 'bout ship in a hurry, I simply shouted, "Full House! Aces High!" and we came round so fast that you hardly knew whether you were on your bowsprit or your starn.

'True? My dear fellow, of course it's true. I am surprised that you should make such a remark.

'Yes, by jove, we had some stirring times on board the *Queen of the West* barque. Curiously enough, her owners in Liverpool renamed her the *Queen of Hearts* after that voyage.'

10 Royal Yacht Squadron

BUT there; the whole screw-sail argument has been most illuminatingly epitomized in the experience of the Royal Yacht Squadron.

In 1827—No! Perhaps we should glance back even farther. For although the history and proceedings of this perhaps too-famous club occupy so much space in yachting literature, there may be here and there some reader unacquainted with its origin, which they may find to have, as I confess it has for me, a kind of antique charm.

Among the folk of means and leisure who could indulge in the new vogue for summer seaside holidays, Cowes first became noted for the quality of its sea-bathing (superior then, one must suppose, to what it is today). 'The locals', on the other hand, employed *their* leisure in racing their fast fishing vessels and pilot-cutters, ferries, and such sort. It being the most natural thing in the world to wish to share in such fine enjoyment and sport, the visitors began hiring boats, and presently to build them. So that there grew up among the summer society at Cowes what one might call a 'salt-water section'.

One day in the year 1815, at the Thatched House Tavern in London, 42 of these enthusiasts met together and constituted their club, the 'Yacht Club', simply, or for better distinction, the 'Yacht Club at Cowes'. It flourished; at first only steadily, but presently more spectacularly, gaining the patronage of the Prince Regent, and so, in 1820, enabled to tack on 'Royal' to its name. Rather later, in 1833, by favour of King William IV, it became the 'Royal Yacht Squadron'.

There was already in the club minutes, however, this famous resolution:

'Resolved that, as a material object of this club is to promote seamanship and the improvements of sailing vessels, to which the application of steam-engines is inimical, no vessel propelled by steam shall be admitted into the club, and any member applying a steam-engine to his yacht shall be disqualified thereby and cease to be a member.'

And right manfully did the Squadron stick to its resolution, to the point of expelling machine-minded members—among them, by the way, Assheton Smith, who with the brothers Napier, was a pioneer of steamer construction and the owner from time to time of no less than nine steam yachts (four of them happily named *Fire Queen*!).

More remarkable still, this ban was maintained from 1827 to about 1851; the clock successfully kept back, so to speak, for a quarter of a century. By the close of that century more than half the Squadron's tonnage was in steam. And such steamers too! 800 tons, 1,000 tons, 1,500 tons, and was to rise still higher until the gathering of the clouds of the First World War.

The Squadron's recision or recantation is, in a way, a more famous and important event in yachting history that the resolution itself. For even today you may hear it debated whether it might not have been a healthier thing for yachting if the Squadron had held out.

For example, sometime between the two world wars a reviewer in *The Times Literary Supplement*—who from strong internal evidence was undoubtedly the beloved 'Q'—quoted with irritation from some yachting book or other in which the author had thoughtlessly claimed for the R.Y.S. that it was the 'greatest power' in yachting.

'*This is nonsense!*' cried 'Q' (if it was he). 'The Squadron, which is mainly a social affair, lost its great opportunity when it admitted mechanically propelled craft.'

Speaking for myself, I would dare to ask leave of 'Q' to doubt both assertions. For the one part, could any club survive as an *enclave*, or sort of artificial preserve—as of birds or game! 'No Admittance' with an engine. For the other part, one could suggest that the Squadron is not so much social as anti-social. What does it say about itself? Pray listen to this from a reputable history:

'In England a thing is valued in proportion as others are prevented from enjoying it.' (*Memorials of the Royal Yacht Squadron*. John Murray, 1902.)

Why, one has known men who have come to Cowes, bought a house, bought a yacht, put up for the Squadron; and then, black-balled, sell the house, sell the yacht, and sink out of sight, believe it or not, *broken-hearted*!

But once inside it is incomparably the nicest club in the world. I say, once inside. . . .

When I was living in London some years ago I was asked whether on behalf of a foreign yachtsman I would assist in taking to Cowes a six-metre yacht which was entered for the Cowes Week regattas. The boat had been unloaded at Southampton, where she was waiting with two or three amateur members of the crew.

I daresay we were not all of us in the best of good humours when we reached Cowes—through my fault we stuck in the mud for ten minutes or so off Calshot—and at Cowes that evening the weather was wretched, gloomy and cold and pouring with rain.

I took my new friends to the yacht club to which I belonged and found it, as it not infrequently is, wholly deserted; not a soul there except the steward. But besides all this I knew perfectly well that where these gentlemen should be presented was the Royal Yacht Squadron.

Out, then, into the rain.

At the porter's lodge I explained our business. At this distance of time I cannot be certain that the signalman was the legendary Wagstaffe himself. Whoever it was, after listening to our story, without comment, but with an air of disbelief, he departed within the precincts. We waited.

He returned, some ten minutes later, requesting us

to accompany him; and our small party advanced up the drive.

When the door opened, bathing us in a warm glow of light, a man within, dressed in a steward's rig-out, asked who we were and what we wanted. Again I said that our boat was entered for the R.Y.S. regattas, that if they were available it would be helpful to receive a programme, and that, as these gentlemen were from abroad, it would be—er—well—nice if one or two other points could be made plain to them.

The man withdrew. Withdrawn also was the warm glow of light, for he had closed the door. But quite shortly he reapp—but no! This was another man, and quite evidently a grade or so superior.

'What was the name of the boat, did we say?

'The *Noreg*.'

'*Noreg? Noreg?* Well, what's the owner's name?'

'Prince Olaf of Norway.'

Our interlocutor vanished.

Two minutes later my new friends and I were on the platform, as this famous room is misleadingly called, being successively introduced, for dinner was just over, to much the most charming men that we had ever met in all our lives.

But, that this expression may have the stricter veracity, I ought rather to say that *I* was never so charmed in *my* life.

I don't know how the members themselves regard Cowes Week, the more anti-social among them, I mean; Cowes Week, which wars against the spirit of

Eternal Wave; Cowes Week, with—'Q' again, if it was he—'its intolerable tittle-tattle and gossip'.

Like many another place, Cowes looks its very best when there is no one about.

In part-illustration, the following yarn may, I trust, be told without hurt to any feelings, since of the persons concerned I alone am still living.

There was, however, on this occasion one person about, Sir Philip Hunloke, the commodore, with whom that season I had been so fortunate as to go sailing in *Britannia*.

'Can you come this evening and dine with me in the club', he asked, after we had briefly recalled these happy experiences.

In the club, also, there was no one about. No! For presently, as we sipped some sherry with our backs to a crackling fire, I observed that there was a man over by a table in one of the corners, silently, but in what appeared to be an absent-minded manner, skipping through the magazines.

Dinner being announced, this other member, a slight, elderly, inconspicuous figure, not to be readily otherwise described, silently entered the dining-room. When we followed, three or four minutes later, he was again seated in a corner, while our table, the commodore's special one perhaps, was in the exact centre of the room.

Try as one may, it is not possible to describe Sir Philip Hunloke by other than the words 'the perfect host'; and I don't believe that I can have ever enjoyed a better dinner, or been more amused, entertained, and instructed, by the conversation of my host.

This memorable repast could scarcely have been

half-way through, however, when the solitary diner in the corner, his meal completed, rose and stole out of the room, *tip-toeing* as it were.

These proceedings were altogether too much for my curiosity and I could not help asking Sir Philip who this third person might be.

'Eh? Who? Oh, some dam' feller. We elected him *thinking he was his brother*!'

11 West-About to Norway

IN the summer of 1933 Dinwiddy and Bartlett took
Eternal Wave to Norway again. This time the voyage
was made west-about, which of course means sailing
up the western coasts of England and Scotland before
crossing the North Sea; a longer route and one of
more general difficulty, needless to say.

A start was made from Dartmouth on June 12.
On the way north the chief ports of call were Scilly,
Douglas, Iona, Stornoway, and from thence to Lerwick, from where the long open-sea passage of 266
miles to Sogn Fjord, Norway, was begun.

This Lerwick–Sogn Fjord passage was the worst
Eternal Wave ever encountered. Dinwiddy's log
describes it as follows:

'*June 27.* Off Haaf Gruney Island—the glass being
steady, the wind N.E. moderate to fresh, and the sky
cloudy to fine but looking settled—it was decided to
set the course for Norway and *Eternal Wave's* head was
put to 97½° for the Sogn Fjord entrance. At 22.40 the
sun set and there was a moderate light through the
short night.

'Through the late evening and the night the wind

increased and was blowing hard N.E'ly, making a big rough sea in which *Eternal Wave* plunged, and, in its rather forward position of the wheelhouse and without the steadying effect of sail, the compass was very unsteady, and the keeping of a course between its semi-lucid intervals was much by the direction of the seas, and by the position of the sun.

'It was fine through the night and morning, the sun setting and rising clear, and the sky without sign of wind clouds but with a glaring brassy appearance. The wind continued very strong and the sea rough, with waves that peaked indiscriminately, broke, and went their way surging until finding their equilibrium again, and there was the occasional combination of seas that broke with more force and surge than others.

'*June 28.* I had been reluctant to reduce speed so long as *Eternal Wave* was making possible weather— and though tossed and lively, she was making on the whole fairly good weather—but after hitting two successive seas with heavy pounding, and extra heavy weights of water coming aboard, necessity called for half-speed, and at 10.30 speed was reduced and *Eternal Wave* made better weather, but the wind and sea continued unabated through the afternoon and into the evening.'

I cannot guess what effect the above piece has on other readers. With me the impression is that Dinwiddy himself was not on board! Far otherwise with Bartlett, who sums up in one vivid sentence:

*The plain unvarnished incident
That actually occurred.*

'When 30 miles out a northerly gale compelled us to heave-to for 14 hours, and *Eternal Wave* was very uncomfortable. And when I saw Mr. Dinwiddy on the wheelhouse floor, tired and wouldn't give in, I thought of those words "Those who go to sea for pleasure ought to go to Hell for pastime".'

'By 23.00 the wind had eased, there was still a big sea, but there was not the drive in it.

'*June 29.* The sea was less and we were able to put the engine to full-speed again. At 01.40 one cylinder was missing, the engine having run non-stop for 40 hours, but after stopping and cleaning the plugs we were under way again within a few minutes.'

After such a dusting, how welcome was the landfall! Dinwiddy describes it with more feeling than usual; indeed it would seem that Norwegian waters had, on this cruise, more than usual charm for him, and he gives many pleasing descriptive entries.

'*Landfall.* At 02.15 judging that sufficient contingent correction to the S. had been made, course was altered to E. by S., and not long afterwards land was made out ahead, at first hardly distinguishable from a cloud-bank, and we finally made the land with its chain of islands, between which we found a passage connecting with Hjelte Fjord, but, due to the anxiety of doubt in the reliability of the unsteady compass, some 20 miles to the southward of the Sogn Fjord entrance proper.

'It was a fine morning—the wind now N. light and

78

the barometer, which had remained fairly steady all through, 29·80—and at 05.30 we made fast alongside a small wharf-staging in a perfect little haven, an enclosed lake with clear blue water and small islands, and to the surprise of the few inhabitants of the scattered hamlet ashore, one or two of whom, as invariably was the experience, had some knowledge of English.

'By the weather map seen later, there has been for the past days a high barometer to the W. of Shetland, and a low to the E. of Sweden, and the wind at 19.00 on Monday, Tuesday, and Wednesday was shown at Shetland 21, 15, and 21 miles an hour, and at sea off Sogn Fjord entrance 35 miles an hour each day. It was through the forenoon and afternoon of Wednesday that the wind and sea were greatest.

'We tidied ship a little after a rather strenuous passage and I had a short walk ashore; after breakfast, intent on making good the objective of the passage into Sogn Fjord, we were under weigh at 10.00 and proceeded northerly up the calm water of Hjelte Fjord. At 11.30 the wind began to freshen again, and later for about two hours, blowing strongly N. in the open approach to Sogn Fjord, it was necessary to reduce to half-speed.

'We continued up Sogn Fjord for some miles, the sea rather rough coming through the many passages between the islands to the northward, and at 19.50 anchored at Bo Fjord, a small inlet on the north side, in 7 fathoms in delightful surroundings, finding a clear passage between rocks by the boat ahead—distance from Lerwick, 266 miles. I walked ashore round the head of the fjord for an hour to Bo Village, very prettily situated on the bank of a rock-strewn stream.

'Several days were spent exploring Sogn Fjord and its shores, and some of its long sea arms running into the mountains which rise precipitately from sea-level, with, in places, little hamlets and larger settlements grouped wherever there is a fertile patch along the shores at the mountain foot, and snow still remained on the mountain tops.

'The water is deep, up to 660 fathoms, in a width which, by the great scale and grandeur of the landscape, appeared very much less than its actual 2 miles. There are anchoring soundings in places, and if not detailed on the chart they can often be found off the shore of a valley's end, or at the head of short indentations in the coast where generally a mountain stream comes down. But, so much are the fjords the only highway for all local traffic by the chugging semi-diesel or diesel, there are landing quays constructed of timber at all the settlements along the coast and often at the smallest hamlets. These enabled us to save the labour of anchor and boat work and the time involved. The tidal rise being only 3 ft. or 4 ft. we lay comfortably alongside; only once in Norwegian waters—and in fact all the way to Dover—using an anchor after leaving Bo, and not once was the boat launched from its housing on deck.

'*June 30*. After making some engine adjustment, we proceeded up the great main fjord from Bo. It was a day of misty rain and cloud on the mountains, which was not without its picturesque effect. In the early evening we made fast at Viksjoren, quite an important settlement, with its houses all typically of wood, at the head of a deep bay on the south side, and looking up a wide bend in the fjord to fine mountain scenery.

'*July 1.* We proceeded northward to Balholm, getting away a little before intended as there was a disturbance by trading boats coming alongside, and when clear we let *Eternal Wave* drift during breakfast. Then we passed, in a wide open part of the fjord, many fishing boats working seine nets for the Norwegian sardine fishery. After a walk ashore at Balholm we continued up the fjord—the wind S.W. fresh and still overcast with cloud on the mountains—then turned southerly into and through the 15 miles of the dark and narrow Naero Fjord, its precipitous mountain sides rising high above. At 18.24 made fast alongside the quay at Gudvangen, intending to remain there for the week-end.

'*July 2.* But there was depression in the shut-in location, deep under the overpowering mountains, and in the morning we got under way at 05.10—a fine morning—and proceeded down Naero Fjord and then down Sogn Fjord (exchanging salute in passing with the Royal Yacht *Prince Olaf*) and turned into Fjaerlands Fjord to the northward at 09.23, against a fresh N.W'ly wind. Continuing up the fjord, with fine views of the mountains and of the glaciers beyond its head, we made fast at Mundal at 11.20. The sky was overcast and it rained heavily in the evening.

'*July 3.* A fine day; we remained at Mundal and I took Bartlett a few miles up the pretty valley set in the mountains to see the Bojumsbrae glacier—an impressive experience.

'*July 4.* We were under way at 06.35 and proceeded down Fjaerlands Fjord and the main Sogn Fjord to Vadheim, making fast there at 12.31; raining, with low cloud and poor visibility.

'In the afternoon I walked some way up a steep road engineered in the mountain side with fine views, and after dinner ashore—an invariable procedure on an evening in port, and which inferred no slight on the excellent working of the ship's galley, and the fresh provisions that it was found possible to keep supplied all through—we cast off again at 21.32, bound for Bergen.

'The wind was S.W. light, there was low cloud and the visibility poor, and proceeding down Sogn Fjord the cloud came lower, hanging like wool in the semi-light of the northern night, only feet above the water; and I decided to find an anchorage. Carrying on, we turned into Risne Fjord, an inlet on the south side, and anchored on its west side just within the entrance at midnight, find with the lead 4 fathoms. The low cloud was now very thick, with fog patches on the water.'

On the following day, during the afternoon of July 5, after an exacting and tiring passage of 132 miles, *Eternal Wave* reached Bergen, the most northerly point of the cruise.

She was 23 days out from England, and had logged 1,429 miles.

A two-day stay at Bergen was made the more enjoyable by fine warm weather, during which the vessel was refuelled and provisioned.

Being now homeward-bound, but seemingly in no haste to reach home, Dinwiddy decided on the unusual course of sailing *eastward* through Lim Fjord, and so into the Baltic and down to Kiel, and from thence out into the North Sea.

This entailed the longest passage of the whole cruise, Bergen-to-Struer, 293 miles, which *Eternal Wave* accomplished in just on forty-eight hours.

Lim Fjord never fails to enchant those who attempt its passage (its western approaches are dangerous in bad weather), so let us here make another pier-head jump aboard *Eternal Wave*.

'*July 9*. At 05.20 we made the W. entrance to Lim Fjord, glad to have the fortune of fine weather . . . and proceeded through Thyboron Channel, of 4 metres least depth and well-marked in the familiar Danish system, for some four miles between shallows.

'We remained at Struer through the day, the British ensign unseen there before in the harbour-master's memory. The town was *en fête*, swimming and other sports all day, and a big gathering of all the countryside.

'*July 10*. Made fast in the harbour of Nykjobing after short passage of 23 miles. Signs of fine weather breaking.

'*July 11*. Thick rain and visibility very poor. Proceeding E'ly for 14 miles across the open water of Logstor Bredning—at the E. end of which the port-and-starboard buoyage system changed, to read outward instead of inward bound—we continued for about 35 miles through narrow channels, sometimes natural, sometimes dredged to a least depth of 4 metres, running through flats that shallow to inches, and at places to a width of 2 or 3 miles. But the channels are all clearly marked, and with care the pilotage presents no difficulty.

'*Aalborg.* As the city of Aalborg is approached the channel widens, and there are two long bridges, the first of which is very low and replaces an old pontoon bridge, and after a short wait its centre span opened for us. We most cautiously passed under the second bridge, which the mast just cleared. Aalborg is a fine city with a large and busy commercial harbour.

'*July 12.* Under way at 06.15—a fine morning, wind S.W. moderate, barometer 29·72—and continued down the channel, putting in at Hals at 08.30 for mail.

'Hals harbour is very small with a narrow entrance, and it was filled with fishing boats. There being no room to turn, we swung ship alongside. Away at 08.57 and proceeded through the 2½ miles of well-marked channel, its main length dredged through the bar, into the Western Baltic, having left to port and starboard some 200 and more can buoys during the past few days.

'And here I would acknowledge the free facilities of all the Norwegian and Danish waters and harbours—and the Dutch—the courtesy accorded to the club burgee and the ensign of a visiting yacht, and the entire freedom from formalities and restrictions of customs and officialdom.

'Outside at 09.29 course was set 154° for Fornaes Point, the wind freshening to strong S.S.W. with rain squalls, making a steep rough sea on the bow. *Eternal Wave* took much light water aboard. At 16.18 we put into the excellent harbour of Grenaa.

'*Ebeltoft, July 13.* Under way at 03.55 for the Great

Belt and Svendborg—overcast, wind S.W. moderate, barometer 29·77—and course was set 187½°. Soon the wind freshened, and after a heavy rain squall, increased again to very strong, making a sea which necessitated reduced speed; and I decided on making Ebeltoft, where we made fast alongside at 09.00.

'*July 14.* It continued to blow very hard S.W. day and night and through Friday, gale at times. Ebeltoft is an interesting old-fashioned small town, and though anxious to get along, I was glad of the opportunity of seeing it. Also I went by bus to Aarhus, an important commercial centre of Jutland, having the usual good sea across the harbour.

'*Svendborg, July 15.* The wind having eased somewhat, though still fresh S.W., and the sky clearing, with a rising glass, we were under way at 04.58. Svendborg was made by the E. entrance at 16.55. Here I arranged for 173 gallons of standard paraffin— the vaporizing type being unobtainable—and with that aboard we moved to the yacht staging within the harbour. The weather was still not fine, but the barometer had risen steadily to 29·80. We remained a day at Svendborg, so delightfully situated on its Sound.'

And so to Kiel, where *Eternal Wave* was again in waters familiar to her from her Oslo cruise.

The main event during her homeward passage across the North Sea was an extraordinary storm on the night of July 20, when off Borkum.

'*July 19.* Passed through the Kiel Canal, and spent the evening alongside at Brunsbuttel, where some tinkering had to be done in the engine-room. The following day saw us plugging down the widening Elbe estuary. Langeoog coming abeam at 21.00.

'Half an hour later—the wind E., light to moderate —there was bright distant fork-lightning to the N. of W., and a distant dark sky which spread. The fork-lightning steadily increased in extent and intensity, until it was vivid and continuous, shrouding the sky for 16 points from the W.S.W. And so it continued for a full two hours, without thunder. On land or sea I have never seen lightning so constant and intense.

'Then, after thunderous rumblings, the storm broke overhead. Out of the N.W. came a squall of wind, quickly knocking up a rough sea. Torrential rain followed and continued for an hour. We were then some eight miles off Borkum. The heavy rain flattened the sea somewhat, then the wind eased and the storm swept away to the E., still vivid, but gradually fading towards dawn, leaving starlight to the W., and a fine morning followed.'

Making Dover on July 25, *Eternal Wave* lay there for a week 'licking her wounds', having odds and ends repaired, and being painted and varnished—the seas had scoured her as clean as a hound's tooth—and all made shipshape for the return to her home port.

Here she arrived on August 3, after an absence of 51 days, during which she had logged 2,735 miles, at an average speed under all conditions of 6·3 knots, and 'achieved the main objective, the great Norwegian Fjord'.

12 'Nightly Stemming Towards the Pole'

IF the west-about-to-Norway cruise impressed the
Royal Cruising Club, its appreciation was expressed
with characteristic moderation.

'Mr. Dinwiddy's long cruise in *Eternal Wave* stands
by itself', observed Admiral M. Lennon Goldsmith,
R.N., who made the club awards for that year. 'If the
whole object of cruising is to get from A to B, Mr.
Dinwiddy has certainly solved the problem.'

Getting from A to B! Here Admiral Goldsmith hints
at that *malaise* which in a greater or less degree infects
all who travel by mechanical means.

> *He never knows what he has missed,*
> *The tense, unhappy, motorist!*

Even in Dinwiddy's logs do we not get the feeling
of being hustled along? And whatever yacht cruising
is or may be, what it should never become is a hustle.

But it is my opinion that Dinwiddy's 'case' (in the
medical sense) cannot be so simply diagnosed. For one
thing, the famous saying, 'The style is the man', whatever truth it has, is perhaps only true of what in
current slang can be called 'a literary type'; which is

87

quite the last description that could be applied to T.N.D.

Yet I really don't know. We can be misled again by his unwillingness to discuss his own feelings, and his seeming incapacity to do so.

'It has been easy to write straightforward accounts of the actual happenings for the *Journal* in the spirit of fellow-membership. But it is different to write for general consumption, and difficult to write of one's own attempts.'

There you are, his own words. So does it not after all look as if this style was this man?

It can be suggested, too, that the expression 'getting from A to B' disposes of the process much too summarily. Getting from A to B can be as ambitious as resolution likes to make it, and just as arduous as the circumstances dictate; depending, of course, on the difficulties, the dangers, the remoteness—or all three —of position B. But precisely why voyages comparable with *Eternal Wave's* are frequently and successfully made under sail rather than with a marine engine (virtually infallible nowadays) is, though a most interesting speculation, a different and larger question—on which Dinwiddy himself may throw some light in a subsequent chapter. And I do know from an occasional aside in one or two of his letters that Dinwiddy felt some pique at the slight but unmistakable tone of patronage or condescension in references to *Eternal Wave* made by the Royal Cruising Club, or more particularly by some of its leading members.

Could this have influenced him when he planned *Eternal Wave's* great cruise of 1935? Haparanda, at the northernmost extremity of the Gulf of Bothnia, is only just short of the Arctic Circle. How about that for position B!

With Dinwiddy and Eales Bartlett on board, *Eternal Wave* left Brixham on June 1, bound for the Baltic and beyond—by way of the Zuider Zee and the Kiel Canal, 'into waters always delightfully interesting to me'.

This time, however, he confesses to finding the earlier passages rather dull, with the exception of an unpremeditated visit to the tiny island of Urk, in the Zuider Zee, where the ship was weather-bound for a day.

'*June 8.* The wind blew hard W.S.W.; we made Urk in a nasty short sea, but its entrance a little under the lee; it blew a gale; we stayed there for a day, but the stay was not regretted.

'Urk is delightfully interesting, a good harbour, rather full, but there was room for us, and the harbour-master, who has charge of all the Zuider Zee harbours, very accommodating. It is the home port of some 430 trawlers of the picturesque high-bowed type, that work the North Sea during the week, and most of them were in for the week-end; and the fishermen and all the natives wear the old Dutch dress, black from top to toe, relieved only by a silver clasp at the waist, pegtop breeches and stockings. . . . And everywhere the fascinating tinkle of the Dutch bells.'

From Kiel, June 12 (when it was Navy Week there), bound for the biggish Baltic Island of Bornholm, *Eternal Wave* was forced by heavy weather to make for Stubbekobing, in Gron Sund, 'where the harbour is excellent'. Rönne (Bornholm) was reached after a night passage of 95 miles. Bound now for Visby, more heavy weather necessitated a call at Borgholm, in Öland Island, the long, narrow island close inshore off the Swedish coast (in shape so like Long Island, U.S.A.), which Dinwiddy made for by the inshore passage, named Kalmar Sound, for which unfortunately, he had only the small scale general Baltic chart.

'A good harbour, Borgholm, small, but the one town of Öland, with a vast old roofless castle in a commanding position. We remained the next day (June 20), held up by a very strong N.N.E. wind.'

This chance visit to Borgholm had an outcome of immense importance, as will shortly be seen.

Visby, in Gotland, was reached on June 22, after a passage of 77 miles; and Dinwiddy was impressed.

'Visby, its site rising from the sea, with its complete walled fortifications, gateways and towers, Cathedral, and many fine though ruined Gothic churches, its quaint streets, may be considered the most picturesque city of the Baltic, and full of history as, until sacked by the Danes in 1361, the forerunner of Lübeck as the ruling centre of the Hanseatic cities.'

Bound away north for the Gulf of Bothnia, and the celebrated port of Mariehamn at its rock-choked

'Eternal Wave' at Urk

approaches, *Eternal Wave* experienced her 'finest hour', as we may say.

'A perfect day, a perfect night, and a perfect passage. The sun went a red ball into the sea at about 21.00, for two or three hours the whole sky to the northward and westward was deep golden red, reflecting its counterpart in deep colouring in a calm sea, and only gradually fading through the semi-light of the night, the moon rose deep red, and by 02.00 the red glow was deepening again to the rising sun . . .

'After a devious passage of some miles between small islands we made fast at Mariehamn on June 23, remaining the following day in perfect weather, the barometer as high as 30·55, and it was the great northern festival of Midsummer's Day.'

Halcyon weather continued with them through the fairyland of the Finnish Åland islands, 'beautiful in their setting of clear full flood water', the yacht now making for Sebbskär Island and the port of Björneborg, its approaches, again, so rock-strewn that even the chart appals one. But ashore Dinwiddy enjoyed a 'very excellent dinner at a well-appointed hotel, four courses, with good restaurant music, which cost 15 marks' (1s. 4d.).

Away north again, *Eternal Wave* crossed the Gulf slantwise to visit Umeå, in Sweden. The following log-entry relating to this place glosses over an incident, on which, luckily, we have one of Bartlett's pungent comments.

'Umeå is some 10 miles up the estuary of a big river, encumbered by islands and banks. The river was heavily in flood and at the quayside running between 4 and 5 knots.

'After seeing the town in the forenoon, I took a 20-mile bus ride to Vannäs, walked for some miles seeing the great river, its gorge of rapids and much timber-logging, and then, assured as to a return bus, started walking along its road, and continued so for the 32 kilometres—for the bus and I did not meet— and I arrived back on board at 00.15 ravenously hungry.

'Such is the effect of the continuous northern light that at 02.00 the town was still soberly alive, and still there were ten or a dozen natives looking aimlessly aboard the stranger from the quayside.'

Now here is Bartlett's version of the bus story:

'He said to me, "I am going for a long bus-ride, and we shall be ready to get under way at 5.30 in the morning".

'He and that bus had a misunderstanding. He arrived back very late, 2.30 a.m. in the following morning. He said to me, "Some young fellows would have grumbled at what happened—I had to walk 32 kilometres back to the ship." Then he said, "I shall be under way to my time, 5.30 a.m." And we were! *Remarkable, I call it.*'

Zigzagging once more, *Eternal Wave's* next port was Uleåborg, in Finnish waters, near the top of the Gulf, and a convenient jumping-off place for Haparanda itself. We now have a strong feeling of being in outlandish parts, perhaps because of the unfamiliar names. Of Uleåborg itself Dinwiddy remarks, 'A fine town with big open squares and wide streets green with

93

trees, and everywhere, harbour and town, so orderly and so clean like all these northern towns, much of wood but with some fine buildings.

'A leg of lamb in the market cost 2s. 3d.'

(Dinwiddy was what the womenfolk would call a good shopper. But I find that Bartlett has made just this observation. 'When it came to shopping, no woman could beat him. Though Mr. D. didn't believe in waste, everything we had was of the best. If we were in an isolated place and the nearest farm was 3 miles away, we would both go and fetch what we wanted.')

The passage from Uleåborg to Haparanda (72 miles) must have been a horror; though one might need to read the entry through twice before this is borne on one.

'*July 3.* At 03.00 we were under way, proceeding through the 40 miles of the northly marked passage of the Uleåborg entrance and approach, then 14 miles on one clear course, *on which we filled our tanks with fresh water from the sea*, and then 16 miles of close pilotage to Haparanda.

'I knew the Haparanda estuary to be shallow, and the stream from the flooded river ran strongly; the Baltic Pilot gives 3 ft. and Carl Leche 1·5 metres, but I relied on there being something more from the river's flood.

'No buoyage is shown on the chart; there were some buoys half-awash to the stream, others probably were down under, rapids indicated shallows, and it was difficult to see where was the channel.

'As I was deciding to find a billet lower down, by good fortune a local passenger boat of some speed was seen coming up astern, and under both engines we were able to take her lead and follow a winding course in her wake, or on her quarter as her course turns against the stream, against a very strong stream that through the big bridge was banked and surging from the piers. We were alongside at Haparanda at 13.00 (Swedish time).'

Eternal Wave was at her port of destination, 34 days out from Brixham, 1,858 miles made good.

The mariner being Dinwiddy, we expect no comment; but we are surprised and delighted to have five words, powerfully evocative and worth a page description.

'Unlike the other towns, Haparanda (and Tornea, a mile away on the Finnish side) have a *look of north and beyond.*'

Then immediately, or rather the next day (July 4), *Eternal Wave's* bows are turned for home.

As usual with him, he gives the impression that the homeward-bound passage was less eventful, and less interesting than being outward-bound. (Can this be true, or have the appearance of being true, of all home-comings?)

The first major port was Vasa, on the Finnish side; another horrible place to attempt without a pilot, and not less daunting to leave.

'For the rather complex exit to the open sea there are eight lighthouses within a space of $2\frac{3}{4}$ miles, and with their characteristics and coloured sectors a pilot surely must be very well versed'; but their own safety

Dinwiddy ascribed to its being 'also well buoyed—and it was daylight.'

Thence, crossing to Härnösand ('about the only part of clear Swedish coast'), *Eternal Wave* hugged this side of the Gulf out into the Baltic through the Öregrund Narrows. Furusund, Sandhamn, Kalmar, Karlskrona, and Ystad, were ports that marked her progress south-westward down the Swedish coast. And so by way of Stege and Svendborg to Kiel. Here the weather broke, strong south-westerlies and gales keeping *Eternal Wave* storm-bound for three days, (July 26–29). Dover was reached on August 3, when the log showed 3,396 miles.

The log of the Gulf of Bothnia cruise is concluded with information useful to yachtsmen planning a visit to those waters.

'The charts used were Admiralty as far as the approach to Åland Island, with the Dutch chart for the Zuider Zee, and the Baltic general chart (W. and E. sheets) from Kiel. In the Gulf of Bothnia the Admiralty general chart was used, with Finnish or Swedish charts of all the port approaches. For the return passage to Kiel the detailed charts of the Stockholm Skärgård and then the General Baltic chart, and the detailed charts again through Danish waters, with the Danish sheet of the Marstal passage.

'A very useful book is *Swedish Harbours*, by Carl Leche, published in Stockholm but printed in English, giving, besides other information, details of 440 Swedish harbours, with plans of most.

'A yachtsman is assured of much courtesy from Customs and other officials in all the Baltic waters; never have I found a full supply of tobacco and stores questioned or sealing suggested, nor have I been asked a harbour due.'

With the completion of this cruise *Eternal Wave* had voyaged in all 15,400 miles, visiting fourteen different countries.

PART THREE

Running by the Lee

13 *Back to Sail*

FOR this cruise to the Gulf of Bothnia the Royal Cruising Club awarded Dinwiddy the Club Challenge Cup, its principal award. Only once before had a mechanically-driven vessel won the cup—namely, the *Inyoni*, a steam-yacht of 66 tons manned by an amateur crew. Dinwiddy was the more gratified that the award had been made by Claud Worth—'that diehardest of the diehards!' as he called him—who had earlier made it plain that he regarded Dinwiddy's ownership of *Eternal Wave* as a falling from grace.

Both Worth and Dinwiddy are dead, and it may be graceless to wonder if there was at any time, or for long, any antipathy between these two outstanding seamen.

In awarding the Challenge Cup Worth employed this sentence: 'Mr. Dinwiddy has an excellent cruising record in sail, and it is entirely to his credit that, when he found himself no longer able to undertake the more strenuous physical work of a sailing yacht, he should have made long cruises by a motor vessel rather than not at all.'

Dinwiddy's age was 60. Did he construe Claud Worth's published remark as an imputation of premature senility? It could be taken as such. And the facts fit. That winter he disposed of *Eternal Wave*.

'I had done what I set myself', he says in a letter, 'with more or less success, and it gave me much sport, and perhaps some adventure, and another rather different experience of seamanship and intimacy with the sea and its "eternal wave". And always I shall be glad of the experience and the memories she gave me; and perhaps she shook a little that diehardest of the diehards, Claud Worth!'

That same winter, 1935–6, he bought a sailing boat, *to sail single-handed*.

I have asked Eales Bartlett, as the man in the best position to know, what he thought Dinwiddy's main motive may have been. This was his unhesitating reply: 'You ask why Mr. Dinwiddy sailed alone in *Svenska*. For honour, nothing else. Mr. Dinwiddy had one thing in mind. To endure hardship so as to become more outstanding to all who knew him and to be worthy of the position of Vice-Commodore if he could achieve it.'

The reader may recall that when *Eternal Wave* was making passage to Visby bad weather compelled her to take refuge in Borgholm, Öland Island. At the time Dinwiddy told us nothing more. A year passed before he made any reference to what then occurred, which was this:

'When at Borgholm I saw a beamy little boat that

appealed to me much. She was only 20 ft. long, but
every foot was boat, clench-built of oak, with good
bow, and the rounded tumble-home Swedish stern;
and her solidity and the grace of her curves showed an
honest and skilled craftsman's work. I noted, after
enquiry, the name of the builder in my rough log as
Truedsson, at Kuggeboda, though vague as to the
places' whereabouts—later finding it to be between
Karlskrona and Ronneby—and continued on my
cruise.

'Some months after returning home I wrote to the
builder of this little boat asking if he would send me
drawings and an estimate for a boat of the type—a
Blekings Kosterbåt, which is a modification of the
real Koster with its extraordinary flare and beam, of
which many are to be seen on the west coast—7·80
metres (25·5 ft.) long, sending him a sketch of the
suggested internal layout and a note of what was to be
included, but not wanting to impose else on the native
design and construction.

'Drawings, obviously from a working boat-builder's
board, duly arrived with an outline specification and,
after a short correspondence upon some details (getting
the Swedish Chamber of Commerce to interpret for
me), the order for the boat was given, and the suggested terms of payment accepted, in an absolute
confidence, without an enquiry.

'The confidence has been fully justified, for the whole
work is very well done, the sail-making, the electrical
installation, and all fittings, though without any
detailed specification, are excellent and complete, and
at a price which by ordinary standards was indeed
very low.'

I don't think I ever learned what he did give for her; but it may suffice to say that in those years the cost of construction in Baltic countries was one-half to two-thirds of the cost at home.

Yachtsmen have at least this charity towards each other: they do not readily tire of the praises of the other man's beloved. We may, then, continue for another paragraph or so about *Svenska*, as the boat was appropriately named.

'*Svenska*, with her overall length of 25·5 ft., has a beam of 9·33 ft. and a draught of 4 ft.; but the lines are easier than the beam would imply. She is very solidly built of 1-in. oak, copper-fastened to $2\frac{1}{4}$ in. grown frames, with heavy oak floor-boards, oak keel, and oak beams. Although the mast is a heavy 40-ft. spar of native timber stepped through the coach-roof, she later showed that there was no sign of strain, and the boat never made a drop of water above or below. The Bermuda-sloop rig has 377 sq. ft. of sail, with hanked staysail and gunmetal worm-gear roller-reefing. Both halyards are single, without purchase, the weight of the boom keeping the luff taut. The engine is a 6 h.p. Swedish Albin, installed under the cockpit floor. The comfortable cockpit is shaped like the top three-quarter profile of an egg. Below, there being only one bunk, there is ample space; a galley by the companion, a lavatory compartment, and a big wardrobe. She carried a Hudson folding boat; but, such are the amenities of N.E. waters, there was no need to launch it until reaching Cowes, after nearly 1,900 miles.'

'Svenska' building at Kuggeboda

What! Karlkrona to Cowes, 1,900 miles? Taking delivery of a small yacht, and above all with the job to do single-handed, would not you, or I, or anybody else, prayerfully make for home by the shortest route?

But not Dinwiddy. To him it presented the not-to-be-lost opportunity of voyaging through the Göta Canal.

This great system, engineered by our own Telford (1810–32), links Stockholm on the east, or Baltic coast, with Gothenburg—or Göteborg, as Dinwiddy always writes it—on the west coast. The total distance is about 360 miles, taking one through scenery of a most captivating kind. But its main charm for the yachtsman is that the canal, or rather series of canals, serve as links between large lakes, in whose expanses he may refresh himself with sailing before again being confined between canal-banks. As a fact, the length of the Göta Canal proper, its artificial work, is not much more than 50 miles. Still, within this stretch there are 58 locks, representing no small amount of labour for one man alone in a boat.

Dinwiddy took possession of *Svenska* in May (1936) and lived in the pretty hamlet of Kuggeboda for some days under the roof of the patriarchal builder, Herr Truedsson with three generations of his family. Those few days were idyllic. 'It was perfect spring weather and the country lovely, the approach to the boat-yard through forest-wood that was carpeted with anemones and spring flowers.'

Svenska began her maiden trip on May 20. On June 4 she reached Stockholm. Mixed weather, and most intricate pilotage. On this passage *Svenska's* owner developed the single-handed routine to which he always conformed thereafter unless circumstances forebade.

'Single-handed, with of necessity enough to do down below for orderly comfort, as well as taking charge above, mainly in narrow waters, where helm and chart generally needed constant watch; my general idea was to cook a good breakfast, have a light lunch and some tea, and whenever possible to make harbour in the evening for dinner on shore.

'Universally in Sweden, even in the small towns, the *Stadshotel* can be relied on for an excellently cooked and served meal for about two-and-a-half *kronor* (a *kronor* equals one shilling).

'Generally, on making harbour, I stowed sail outside, rigged fenders on each side (excellent white rubber ones that are clean, handy, and quite wearproof), and with head and stern warps in place, went in ready to choose a billet on either hand.'

Having paid the due, 28·80 *kronor* (minimum charge for 10 tons and under) *Svenska* passed through the first three locks on June 9, when, at Söderköping, there was 'the usual excellent dinner on shore'. June 10 she negotiated the 13 locks which space the 11 miles of canal which leads into the small lakes of Asplången and Roxen.

And so day by day, by canal and lake, and canal and lake again, into Vettern, one of the big lakes, 65 miles along its longer axis, which Dinwiddy explored with some thoroughness, fetching up of an evening alongside in some old town with an ancient Gothic castle or cathedral, in sight of which to enjoy 'the usual excellent dinner'.

On June 17 man and boat were at Lake Viken,

which marks the 'divide', the lock here being the last rising lock 300 ft. (91·4 metres) above sea-level; and so, presently, into the great lake of Vänern, in which Dinwiddy sailed about happily for some days, visiting, among other places, Kristinehamn.

'Here was the home of my Albin engine, which had behaved without falter, and did all through the cruise, but I was vague as to much about it, and one of the directors of the maker company came aboard and gave very useful service. There were a number of yachts in the harbour, but hundreds of day motor-boats, moored in tiers, all very shapely, sturdy boats, typically double-ended and with a pronounced sheer.'

Svenska reached the south-western extremity of Lake Vänern on June 22. Here the Göta River flows to Gothenburg and the sea, at the Cattegat, a length of something under 50 miles, part of which is canalized. To begin with the Göta flows through Tröllhattan, famous for its falls and rapids, through which, in less than a mile, the river falls 108 ft. Harnessed, this great power, 18,000 cu. ft. a second, serves mills and factories and provides electricity to many towns including Gothenburg. It much impressed Dinwiddy, who 'walked to the falls and saw and heard the roar of the terrific power of the spring water from the great lake'.

Svenska lay the next night at Kungalv, an old and picturesque little river-port, and afterwards negotiated the rest of the passage without incident.

At Gothenburg a comparatively peaceful mooring

was found alongside piles in the Fish Harbour, where, in the 'Doctor-Livingstone-I-presume' manner in which R.C.C. members so much delight, Dinwiddy found the English yacht *Albatross* with Colonel H. E. Gunn ('of the Club') aboard.

Bound now for home by way of Copenhagen and the Kiel Canal, Dinwiddy was again in waters which he had thrice visited in *Eternal Wave*.

What so wretchedly distinguished the passage home was the appalling weather. (Somewhat later that summer the big Elbe No. 1 Lightship foundered at her mooring with the loss of all hands.) *Svenska* was in those waters in mid-July. Storm-bound in Cuxhaven for four days, she set out on July 17, and within a few hours Dinwiddy was in a situation of no small peril.

'*July 18.* At 03.40 course was altered to S. 85° W. for Terschelling. The wind soon freshened, there were heavy clouds to the southward with evidently something coming, and a little later, just as I had completed rolling two reefs in the mainsail, a very heavy squall was seen approaching from the south, with a muddy-greenish line across the water. Hove-to on port tack, it came with deluging rain and incessant thunder, and for an hour it blew harder than I have known at sea.

'*Svenska*, with the 75 sq. ft. of staysail a-weather, and main sheet slacked right off, lay over to her rail, as I tended the helm, generally hard down, with a turn of the weather tiller line round my left hand. The servings of the three top hanks of the mainsail luff carried away, putting great strain on the fourth, which held. But the topping lift carried away chafed through at the boom-end.

'When the storm eased, I lowered the damaged sail, lashed the boom, and started the engine: but it would do little against the wind (which had veered W.S.W.), and the sea and ebb-stream which were then running. Loth to lose anything that had been made good to windward, I decided to make Borkum, which would give a fair wind and the stream with it. Visibility was poor, but I found the outer buoys to the Hubert Gat, the next buoys not being visible from them, and ran the 17 miles to the small harbour that is tucked away round the southern point, and was alongside at 10.40.'

On August 14, 96 days out from Kuggeboda-Karlskrona, *Svenska* picked up *Eternal Wave's* old moorings in the River Dart. Single-handed, her owner had logged 2,000 miles, visited 60 ports—'I managed to explore ashore all the places where I put in'—on a cruise which, for ardours and skill, makes the crossing of an ocean, Atlantic or any other, appear simple in the comparison.

Svenska's owner was 'without hesitation' awarded the R.C.C. Club Challenge Cup, the first member to have won the chief award in two successive seasons.

14 Single-handed

IN all the countries we regard as the most civilized,
men attempt the most fantastic deeds to assure
themselves that they are still men, and not nameless,
minute, redundant parts in a vast, universal, and
incomprehensible machine.

They race motor-cars round concrete tracks for days
and nights on end. They swim seas and channels.
They fly round the world to no purpose whatsoever.
They have climbed all the mountains. They have
stood at both the Poles. Now they speculate about the
stratosphere and beyond.

But there remains, and at hand, so to speak, one
unconquered and unconquerable territory—the sea.
Disfigure the land as he may, man can mark no right
of way across the sea. The sea paths are obliterated
the instant each keel has passed. Pure, stainless,
inscrutable sea!

'The sea!' cried Herman Melville. 'It is the image
of the ungraspable phantom of life; and this is the key
to it all.'

All this is a high-falutin' way of saying that there is no exhausting the adventure of seafaring, no end to the enchantments of the sea. It follows then that those who seek the deepest experiences must be dedicated souls, single-minded. From whence also it follows that such men will tend, or be drawn to, or prefer—whatever the right word may be—single-handed sailing.

Talking somewhere of monasteries and nunneries and those who occupy them, Anatole France speaks of 'claustral souls'—folk whose mentality finds more nourishment, and their spirits a more congenial earthly home, in associations which have the fewest contacts with the everyday world. Anatole France maintained (if I recollect aright) that this withdrawn temperament was of a special and recognizable kind, and fairly widespread.

In people of the British race, however, the meditative side of the character seeks, paradoxically, a practical manifestation. Even while allowing for the inconvenient scarcity of monasteries and nunneries to which to flee the world—that part of it in the British Isles—it would seem that we are not a folk which takes kindly to any description of immuring walls. Hence, having not much inclination or aptitude for the world as it daily presents itself, British people of this cast of mind do appear to prefer the wild places, taking to the privations of the ice, the sea, the desert, the mountains, or the jungle, as claustral souls of other races take to their penances and prayers.

But there we go again, more high-falutin'! One, might have said it all with one phrase from Kipling, just calling it the 'I must get 'ence' mood.

My own experience of single-handed sailing has been so short and slight, a mere pottering extending not much beyond the creeks and waters of the Solent, that to mention it at all would be presumptuous, did not honesty compel the admission that it is the sort of adventure that I vastly prefer above all others, and so make it clear that in this matter I am on the side of what in my regard are—as the foregoing paragraphs have hinted—the angels!

So then, and rather, let us listen to a man qualified to speak not only from his experience but also with an eloquence and humour that are charming and delightful. This man is the Marquis of Dufferin and Ava. And his paper on 'Single-Handed Sailing' appeared in the second of the two yachting volumes in the Badminton Library. It has dismayed me to discover lately how little this famous essay appears to be known among the past couple of generations of yachtsmen, for the volumes have been reprinted from time to time since their first issue in 1893–4; although, one must in fairness mention, no more than one edition, has, I think, been reprinted in this present century.

Lord Dufferin was possibly the first to speak up for single-handed sailing, but it may be more certainly claimed that on this subject he has, as the phrase is, said the last word.

So we may treat ourselves to an extract or two for our own enjoyment as well as giving the younger hands what used to be quite properly called a 'whet'.

Needless to say, Lord Dufferin began his yachting in a big vessel with a brass-bound skipper and professional crew. The essay describes, in felicitous phrases, what this felt like to him.

'. . . No Emperor or autocrat has ever been so conscious of his own majesty. But soon a most unwelcome and humiliating conviction damps his exaltation. He discovers that for all practical purposes and of command and government he is more incompetent than his own cabin-boy or the cook's mate; that the real ruler of the ship's movements and destiny is his "master", whom his crew call the "captain"; and that the only orders he can give with a certainty that they are not open to criticism are those which he gives for his breakfast and his dinner, if indeed he is in a position to partake of either. Officially he is gratified with the ambiguous title of "owner", while he is painfully conscious that his real status is that of a mere passenger, and that this unwelcome servitude has every likelihood of enduring during his whole career as a yachtsman . . .

'But in single-handed sailing this humiliating sense of dependence and inferiority disappears. For the first time in his life he finds himself . . . with that delightful sense of unlimited responsibility and co-extensive omnipotence which is the acme of human enjoyment.

'All the problems which tax the intelligence and the knowledge of the captain of a thousand-tonner during the various contingencies of its nautical manœuvres have to be dealt with by him with equal promptitude and precision. Anchored in a hot tideway and among a crowd of other shipping, he has perhaps a more difficult job to execute in avoiding disaster when getting under way or picking up his moorings than often confronts under similar circumstances the leviathans of the deep; and his honour is equally engaged in avoiding the slightest graze or sixpence worth of injury either to himself or his neighbours as would be the case were a court-martial or a lawsuit and £5,000 damages involved in the misadventure.

'The same pleasurable sentiments stimulate his faculties when encountering the heavy weather that awaits him outside.

'Nor are even misfortunes when they occur, as occur they must, utterly devoid of some compensating joys. He has neglected to keep his lead going when approaching land; he has misread the perverse mysteries of the tides, and his vessel and his heart stop simultaneously as her keel ploughs into a sandbank.

'The situation is undoubtedly depressing, but at least there is no one on board, on this and on similar occasions to eye him with contemptuous superiority or utter the aggravating "I told you so". Nay, if he is in luck, the silent sea and sky are the only witnesses of his shame, and even the sense of this soon becomes lost and buried in the ecstasy of applying the various devices necessary to free his vessel from her imprisonment. He launches his Berthon boat and lays out an anchor in a frenzy of delightful excitement; he puts into motion his tackles, his gipsy winches, and all the mechanical appliances with which his ingenuity has furnished his beloved; and when at last, with staysail-sheet a-weather, she sidles into deep water, though, as in the case of Lancelot, "his honour rooted in dishonour stood", the tragic origin of his present trial quickly fades into oblivion, and during after-years he only recalls to his mind, or relates with pride to his friends, the later incidents of the drama.

'Another happiness attending his pursuit is that he is always learning something new. Every day, and every hour of the day, the elements of each successive problem with which he has to deal are perpetually changing. As Titian said of painting, seamanship is an art whose horizon is always extending: and what can be more agreeable than to be constantly learning something new in a pursuit one loves?

'. . . In conclusion, I would submit that to anyone wearied with the business, the pleasures, the politics, or the ordinary worries of life, there is no such harbour of refuge and repose as single-handed sailing. When your whole thoughts are intent on the management of your vessel, and the pulling of the right instead of the wrong string, it is impossible to think either of your breakdown in your maiden speech in the House of Commons, of your tailor's bills, or of the young lady who has jilted you.

'On the other hand, Nature, in all her beauty and majesty, reasserts her supremacy, and claims you for her own, soothing your irritated nerves, and pouring balm over your lacerated feelings. The complicated mysteries of existence reassume their primeval symplicity, while the freshness and triumphant joyousness of early youth return upon you as you sweep in a dream past the magic headlands and islands of the Ionian Sea or glide along the Southern coast of your native land, with its sweet English homes, its little red brick villages and homesteads nestling in repose amid the soft outlines of the dear and familiar landscape. The loveliness of earth, sea, and sky take possession of your soul, and your heart returns thanks for the gift of so much exquisite enjoyment in the pursuit of an amusement as manly as it is innocent.'

Is not this as true as it is charming?

'. . . *All the mechanical appliances with which his ingenuity has furnished his beloved.*'

Does one expect an extraordinary man to possess an extraordinary yacht? At any rate, Lord Dufferin, a man of extraordinary talents, owned a most extraordinary single-hander. *The Lady Hermione*, built at Wivenhoe somewhere prior to 1890, was a gaff-rigged yawl, straight stem, counter stern, with a long bowsprit. In nothing else was she normal. She was only 24 ft. on the waterline, yet internally she was boxed in with steel bulkheads; four of them. She was ballasted with two tons of lead, most of it outside. On top of that, or rather underneath it, a heavy oak keel was fitted to make her stand up to her sail. Conceive of it! She must have been, for her size, the heaviest displacement vessel in the history of naval architecture. Yet she was a success, and her owner sailed her safely in home and foreign waters.

The great principle in 'all the mechanical appliances with which his ingenuity furnished' *The Lady Hermione* was that her solitary occupant should be able to do everything from the cockpit. Everything. All the sheets and halyards led aft—main and peak halyards; two topping-lifts; tack tackle and tack-tricing line; topsail tack, sheets, halyard and clew line; jib and staysail halyards; and jib and staysail downhauls—to name some, and each with its gunmetal sheaves and tally-plate—the anchor could be let go and heaved in—and in deed as well as in theory all could be done from the cockpit; for even the Berthon boat was stowed in the cabin. Sometimes she was steered with a tiller, sometimes with a wheel; it depended on whether Lord Dufferin was sailing with a lady companion (for he held that 'single-handed sailing need not preclude the presence of a lady *passenger*'). And if a lady was on board he then brought into action an elaborate fitting which held a nicely adjustable parasol.

But even to attempt to describe *The Lady Hermione* as she deserves would take pages. 'It's like being inside a clock', was how a naval officer summed her up, while another said she was a 'mosaic of ingenuity'.

What a man, was this first marquis of Dufferin and Ava!

An obituary notice anonymously contributed to the first volume of *The Yachting Monthly* (1906) says of him that he endeared himself to everyone he ever met, and adds this sentence (remarkable, by the way, for its skilful alliteration): 'The personal magnetism and charm of manner, the genius, generosity, geniality, the courage, candour, culture, tact, and taste of the man, cold print were as impotent to convey as to reproduce the fragrance of a flower!'

Dufferin's mother was a descendant of Richard Brinsley Sheridan; and it was to the distaff side that Dufferin's dazzling gifts as well as his highly distinguished looks were most generally attributed. But surely the strength and sweetness of his *character* owed as much to the seafaring Blackwoods. His uncle was that Sir Henry Blackwood, one of the 'band of brothers', the 'God bless you, Blackwood' of the last hour of Trafalgar. Dufferin's own father was Captain Price Blackwood, R.N., of whom it had been said, 'A thorough sailor, frank and open, the soul of honour, with the kindest heart I ever knew'.

15 Running by the Lee

I TRUST that admiration for the subject of our last chapter did not convey the suggestion that Lord Dufferin was the pioneer of single-handed sailing. This is a distinction which most yachtsmen attribute to R. T. McMullen. Though if the point were to be decided strictly on seniority, I believe there to be enough evidence to decide it in favour of Frank Cowper.

However this may be, McMullen's exploits were the first to be published. And, moreover, his few and early writings became the gospel, in the sense of the 'good news', for single-handers; teaching, above all, that provided she was well-found and well-handled, and kept *away* from the land in bad weather, a small ship was as safe as a vessel hundreds of times her size. It is perhaps impossible to exaggerate the comfort—to put it as low as that—which this great truth has brought to cruising yachtsmen in the three or four generations that have sailed the seas in small craft since McMullen's time.

In 1857 McMullen sailed the 3-ton *Leo* from Greenwich to Land's End. He was accompanied by a boy. But 'no one but myself knew whither I was bound, not even the boy'.

In the seasons following McMullen set himself deliberately to acquire the hardihood and skill essential in a single-hander. 'I envied the bargemen', he said, 'their coolness and evident self-possession, and I looked forward to the time when I should feel the same confidence. My plan was to persevere in sailing by day or night in all weathers, and never let the want of confidence stand in the way. In this manner, getting into scrapes and getting out of them, I learnt more of practical sailing in a few months than I should have learnt in several years if I had hired a man to take the lead in everything.'

Perhaps the reader has already observed that McMullen avoids the use of the word 'yachting'. He preferred the term 'yacht sailing'. 'If I may compare sailing with equestrian sports, I should say that yacht sailing stands in about the same relation to yachting as the hunting-field does to Rotten Row.'

There will be few, one fancies, who will not pause here, reflecting how often they have been struck with the insufficiencies of this word 'yachting' to describe the manifold joys and tribulations of amateur seafaring!

What one most objects to in the word is its connotation of wealth, luxury, brass-work, Cowes Week, and the rest of it; though with all of this, to be sure, yachting has less and less to do. Still we are shy of the word, and steer round it with 'sailing' and 'my old boat'.

This strange word 'yachting', with its soft look and hard sound, is the anglicized form of *jacht*, from the Dutch *jaghen*, to hunt or pursue, and was originally applied to any fast, small sailing vessel in the Low Countries; and thus the expression 'private yacht' is not so tautological as nowadays it looks and sounds. The word 'yacht' is thought to have been first used in this country by Pepys: 'In the year '60 the Dutch gave his Majesty a yacht called the *Mary* from whence came the improvements of our present yachts; for until that time we had not heard such a name in England.'

In Britain, since Charles II's time, a yacht seems always to have been a private vessel; on which fact, indeed, the earliest definition which one has seen is insistent: 'Built for private pleasure sailing and not plying for hire'. This of course would admit everything from a sailing canoe upwards, and so we later find it implied or stated that the vessel must be covered in, and (more disputably) capable of sea-going.

Much later came Froude's famous definition—Beauty, Habitability, and Speed. Of which one could say these are

> . . . *Sisters,*
> *Never sundered without tears.*

For it has often been observed of this definition that if, say, either speed or habitability is primarily sought, then beauty goes by the board.

But I would also like leave to observe that the less expert, or scientific, the definition is the more amusing it is likely to be. 'A yacht', said the stuffiest member in one of our stuffier clubs, 'is a means of getting away from one's wife, or an inconspicuous way of drinking oneself to death!'

But hear, rather, a man who practised what he preached, Hildebrand, who wrote *Blue Water*. 'In a yacht', says Hildebrand, 'you are at once a wanderer and a stay-at-home. You carry your house with you everywhere, and it carries you. It is the best of houses —a snug, trim habitation, weather-tight, sheltered, and secluded, although the weather itself, wind, rain, and sea, is just outside. It is compact and complete— large enough, yet not too large—neatly kept, since there is no room to have it otherwise, convenient, since disorder and a ship do not agree, resourceful, since you are cut off from the world. To live aboard ship', said Hildebrand 'is the best of lives.'

A yacht! She is wealth's most graceful display, over whose construction hundreds of men in scores of trades have laboured for years. Or she belongs to the working-man who converts a ship's lifeboat with his own hands in his own time in his own backyard. Or she is manned by brass-bound officers and a crew of forty hands. Or she is the single-hander, hove-to in the Channel while the ship's company cooks his own breakfast. She is a yacht!

Hildebrand—dear me, how these names do start one off!—was a young New Englander with a most intense and exclusive obsession for the small sailing vessel. As a matter of tragic and most literal fact, it was the death of him.

He was intended for Dinwiddy's profession, that of architect, but he did not pursue it with Dinwiddy's application and eventual distinction; indeed, he seems not to have pursued it at all, for he shortly abandoned it for a job as librarian to the Yale Club, in New York. Nor did he stick this for long, because a friend held out to him the glittering enticement of a yacht cruise in the Mediterranean. This duly came to pass—at least the pair of them successfully got the *Caltha* (an old-fashioned yawl of about 15 tons) so far as Marseilles—and out of these experiences Hildebrand wrote his book.

Before you are through the first two chapters (which are the best in the book) you realize that you are being enchanted by a writer born. Again, had he stuck to the pen he might have made a career, and certainly a reputation, and almost as certainly prolonged his life; for we learn, unexpectedly, that he was of weak constitution, unfitted for the sort of seafaring for which he had so consuming a passion.

The short sad tale is that, back in New York again, Hildebrand met 'Typhoon' Bill Nutting, an almost legendary figure already, who had recently made a desperate yacht-crossing of the Atlantic. Nutting's plan was to sail from Norway to America by the route believed to have been used by the Norse discoverers, or rather by the most famous of Norse explorers, Leif Ericcson.

Instantly Hildebrand was, as we say, 'mad' on it. The boat was built, *Lief Ericcson* by name, Shetland was reached, and Iceland was reached, but it had been so difficult and laborious a passage that the season was now too far advanced for further progress to the westward to be prudently chanced. Still, they did chance it, and no word more has ever been heard of Hildebrand, Nutting, or the *Lief Ericcson*.

16 Single-handed (Resumed and Concluded)

WE have, I fear, been running by the lee through most of that last chapter, when our proper course should have been more in McMullen's wake.

It is well known that the circumstance that turned McMullen into a single-hander was the series of rows he had with his two paid hands in the *Orion*. Of course, we hear only McMullen's side of the argument; and to me at any rate, with my natural impulse to side with the professionals, it does not seem that the men could always have been in the wrong, though they may have been mainly so. (It is invariably the owners and amateurs who write about yachting. But, with only a few startling exceptions, the classics of sea literature in general have been written by men who served before the mast.)

Of the two men in *Orion*, Henry had sailed with the owner before. The other man was George, whom Henry had recommended. I am inclined to think that the two were not good for each other, or rather that George had a bad influence on Henry, who had shown himself to be an able and willing seaman.

In the slang of today McMullen was 'tough'. He enjoyed what he called 'a smart sail', and preferred to punch to windward rather than to await a favourable slant. On this particular trip in *Orion* he had hoped to reach Cherbourg. Sailing from London River, they met fresh head-winds and had to bring up once or twice on the way to the southward. The men had already begun grumbling, complaining that they were not getting time enough below, although the owner logged that they had $7\frac{1}{2}$ hours on the night they grumbled most.

Off Dungeness, Henry came aft and said that 'it was very hard they could not get their dinner in peace, but must have it spoilt by salt water. McMullen pointed out that the fore-hatch had been left open. But the incident so angered him that he ran back to Dover. 'Running back with a whole mainsail in fine sunny weather was so contemptible that it was enough to make one sick with shame and vexation.' In Dover the owner had it out with the men, who appeared ashamed of themselves and agreed to stick by the ship and take the rough with the smooth.

But matters were soon as bad as ever, and in the end —and in short—the owner offered either to take the men to sea, blow high, blow low, in lieu of a week's wages, and so discharge them in a British port, or he would pay their fare home by steamer. Henry and George chose the steamer.

In due course McMullen sailed the *Orion* home alone.

She was $19\frac{1}{2}$ tons, 48 ft. overall; a deep and narrow cutter, heavily sparred, having a large sail plan, and topsail and squaresail yards, and all the cumbersome gear and paraphernalia which went with a vessel of that type at that time, the year 1877. McMullen was no Goliath, being indeed slight and spare, a David rather, so that his feat was the more considerable.

In the next season, that of '78, he published his little book under the long title of *Orion, Or How I Came To Sail Alone in A 19-Ton Yacht. With Remarks on Collisions and Lighthouses, &c.* This '&c' included tirades in the characteristic McMullen manner against 'Idler's Union', popular education, and tobacco smoking, though there are also other short papers which furnish more profitable matter.

Thereafter McMullen did not devote himself to single-handed sailing exclusively, as we may have been led to suppose, though he did a certain amount, notably in the *Procyon* (7 tons). And of course it is the next best-remembered fact about this undoubtedly great man that, in Dixon Kemp's memorable sentence:

'He died upon the sea, sitting in the cockpit of the little *Perseus*, his face towards the sky, whilst she was sailing up the silver path of the moon which seemed to unite heaven and the sea.'

Scripture somewhere warns us: 'Talk not of other men's lives', so difficult it is, when we fall to gossip, not to spice it with denigration, born of envy and all uncharitableness. Though it is not to point this that I copy out this short reminiscence of Frank Cowper's, who had been to tea in a friend's yacht lying in Bembridge.

'Among other topics touched upon I remember was

McMullen's End

the dislike of Mr. McMullen for snug anchorages, or
even entering harbours. For of course one can understand this, for it is precisely here the greatest difficulties
attend the short-handed man. . . . It is when entering
such places at Havre, Ostend, St. Malo, even Peter
Port, Guernsey, that the single-handed cruiser is put
on her mettle.

'Somebody wanted to know the real extent of Mr.
McMullen's single-handed voyages. Nobody seemed
quite to know, except that he sailed from Cherbourg to
the Thames, where he wired for assistance to help
berth him, that he sailed down Channel in the *Orion*,
where he was found dead somewhere off Cape Levi.
All the other voyages seemed to have been done with
two or three hands. Possibly we did not credit this
brave seaman with a sufficient number of single-
handed cruises.

'There is no doubt his voyage from Cherbourg did
an immense deal to inspirit others to handle craft
larger than usual, and I fully expect to see craft of
from 18 to 22 tons, designed expressly for single-
handed work, being quite common round our coasts.
There is every reason why it should be so . . .'

From that day to this day the yachting journals have
been much occupied with discussion on 'The Ideal
Single-Hander'. Judging by the space accorded it,
no subject arouses more general interest; none is more
unfailingly perennial. To make use of Frank Cowper's
phrase, 'There is every reason why it should be so'.
For one thing, designing being an art, there is no end
to it. Who ever attained perfection? And it is because
we shall never have done with altering, improving,
inventing, and general fiddling about, we have a

happy interest that outlasts all others. And one needn't spend a penny! Why, Johan Anker, to whom we owe the Dragon design among others, did all his work in bed! There's no soporific design like it! Well do we call these visions 'Dream-ships'!

I know of no happier fulfilment of Cowper's prophecy than Arthur Briscoe's *Golden Vanity*.

Now there is a single-hander's actualized dream if you like! To begin with, 21 tons, and a gaff-cutter with 1,100 sq. ft. of canvas. About the same overall as she is on the waterline; 38·8 ft. and 36 ft. And 12 ft. beam, and under that 7 ft. of headroom fore and aft! Designed by A. Gibbs, and built within a biscuit toss of Dinwiddy's place, at Galmpton, by Saunders in 1908. Could a sailor-artist improve on this for a floating studio-home? But then Arthur Briscoe had a wealth of experience on which to plan and build.

Born at Birkenhead in 1873 (a couple of years before Dinwiddy, and like Dinwiddy living to be 70), he had the Mersey at his doorstep. Small wonder that a lad of his nature was fascinated by that matchless panorama, or that, on leaving Shrewsbury, he took to the sea, serving in sail before the mast for many voyages.

During the wander-years he discovered his talent for drawing. To forward this gift, for the time being he swallowed the anchor, studying at the Slade, and then at Julian's, in Paris. From his twenty-third to his twenty-eighth year he painted assiduously, mostly in water-colour, exhibiting at shows in London and up and down the country.

All this while he was sailing in small craft, mostly in East Anglia, and always, as must be with such men, with his artist's eye and hand at work. At one time during this period he got hold of a kind of dumb barge, and made of her something that was a wonder to see. Briscoe gave her 'gun ports', contrived a vast studio-saloon, in which he built a brick fire-place weighing a couple of tons or more, and finally rigged the *Puffin*, as he disarmingly named her, as a schooner.

Once at least he went back to sea again in a square-rigged deepwaterman. On another adventure he cruised extensively through Europe by canal, in a barge rigged with a single vast headsail.

Occasionally he contributed to the yachting press, notably *The Yachting Monthly*, under the name of 'Clove Hitch'. In 1904 Clove Hitch wrote and John Lane published *A Handbook on Sailing*. I have this slim, green, little volume by me now, and I am as charmed now as I was forty years ago by its black-and-white sketches; simple subjects, but beautifully done, and so true in atmosphere as well as in detail that it seems you see the sea and smell the breeze. The influence of this little book must have been enormous. It had so profound an effect on me, it is no more than honest to say, that if I had any doubt that the sailor's life was the right choice for me, Clove Hitch clinched it.

And if I were asked this good long time afterwards what was the thing or theme of special appeal in this truthful little book, I would say that it was the scorn for mere 'yachting'; its pure passion for boats and sailing, rather than the wearisome trappings of the thing. This doctrine of simplicity needs always to be preached. When one hears of any unwholesome tendency in racing or cruising one may usually trace it to the loss of the saving grace of simplicity.

In the War of 1914–18 Briscoe served in the small craft of the R.N.V.R. (Auxiliary Patrol). When it was over he went back to his painting.

Some years afterwards, when he was turned fifty, Arthur Briscoe stumbled into his real life-work. One says 'stumbled', and it was almost exactly that. While clearing a corner of a lot of jumbled gear he came across a copperplate. Contemplating the thing, he felt a strong impulse to try an etching for himself. Within a year he had not only mastered the technique, but had also published six prints of high promise. A few months later he had another half-dozen to show. Among these first-fruits were the now internationally-famous *Up Channel* and, wonderfully beautiful, *Furling the Foresail*.

At this point Briscoe seems to have felt the need to digest this experience and check his bearings, as it were. So off he went deep-sea in sail again. By this time the British square-rigger had all but disappeared from the oceans, and so the vessel he shipped in was a Danish training ship. In her Briscoe, who signed articles as the 'Teacher in English', sailed from Fowey to Genoa. When he reached home again, if it was not to find himself famous, it was certainly to put the finishing touches to the work which earned this fame; for to this period belong the spirited yet delicate masterpieces as *Clewlines and Buntlines*, now so esteemed the world over.

The most striking thing about it all, to my mind, is that Briscoe did not come into his proper place in life until past fifty years of age—'his clock did not chime till then', to use a phrase I heard applied to another man. Is not this a fact of the most heartening sort? For it does appear as though, in the increasing complexity of life, a man is compelled to serve an ever-lengthening apprenticeship.

Thus it can be suggested that Arthur Briscoe's example may be of much comfort to the many whose 'clock has not chimed', because it is another instance of working faithfully on in the belief that the job may come to have a value that one cannot even guess at.

17 Conclusion

TOWARDS dusk on a calm day in mid-autumn—
in 1922 or 1923—my little *Puffin* was drifting up
the Hamble River on the last drain of the flood tide.
Lying moored in the bight of the river at Burlesdon
was a staunch cutter of about 30 tons, a wisp of blue
smoke eddying from her polished 'Charlie Noble'.
Standing by the heel of her bowsprit was a middle-
aged man, slight in figure, with the look of an experienced sailor about him, who, as we drew
abeam, politely hailed:

'That's a very nice little vessel you have there, sir.'

I glanced round, to see what the vessel was, and
who the 'sir' might be. But nothing was stirring, not a
soul was in sight. Surely not, but—could it be?—that
he meant the *Puffin* and I? The 30-ton cutter was
Tern III and the man was Claud Worth.

Claud Worth! How to tell what this meant? It gave
one a glow of happiness that lasted for years. But then,
such an out-of-the-way kindness to a young stranger
was exactly characteristic of Claud Worth, the most
accomplished all-round yachtsman of his time, and
one might even dare say of our times as well.

Worth was a striking example of a child brought up inland, and of land-abiding stock, yet *born*—so mysteriously!—with a great love of the sea. We have his own word for it that he yearned for it from infancy, but that his father (who, in a strange phrase, 'did not believe in the existence of the sea') determinedly saw to it that he should follow some other calling as his profession. The calling that he did adopt was medicine, to become, in time, as is well known, a distinguished ophthalmic surgeon, famous, particularly, for his work among young children.

Worth's yachting career extended from 1880, when at the age of eleven he built himself a successful little boat, until his death fifty-six years later; his last days being occupied with the design and scale-drawings of an 11-ton cutter. Needless to attempt to summarize the crowded years between. 'Are they not written in the book?'—Worth's *Yacht Cruising*.

The influence of that work, now I believe in its fourth edition, has been extensive and profound. Its peculiar merit is that it is a perfect splice of theory and practice: first the *how* and then the *why*; as, say, 'A boat with a cut-away profile will not heave-to *because* . . .' While it's charm resides in the fact that it is a yacht-by-yacht account of the author's own lengthy and ripe experience, pondered by an acute intelligence, and recorded with a clarity amounting to genius.

This is why at times, or for a period, one charges Worth with being pontifical. *The Oracle Speaks.* Be thou dumb! But then to have entertained such a feeling at all is some measure of the man's vast superiority.

Worth could, though, when he cared to—for no

more than Dinwiddy did he wear his heart on his
sleeve—write with tenderness:

'I never make even the most familiar landfall after
days at sea without feeling that I know why men
flocked to the Crusades, why volunteers filled the tiny
ships to conquer and explore the New World, why men
strive to reach the Poles or to penetrate the deserts of
Thibet.

'Hope of gain or glory, duty, patriotism, have each
had a share, but the sense of romance and adventure
and the joy of personal achievement have been the
main incentives to nearly all noble enterprises.

'We who adventure upon the sea, however humbly,
cannot but feel that we are more fortunate than
ordinary people, and that we have something which we
could not tell nor they understand. A love of the sea
with some seems almost innate, to others it may come
late in life; but no man who has loved the sea can
forsake her, ever.'

Claud Worth was Vice-Commodore of the Royal
Cruising Club from 1919 until his death in 1936. He
was succeeded in that office by Dinwiddy, who thus
achieved his ambition; the 'honour'—as Bartlett had
truly sensed—for which he had disciplined himself to
'endure hardship'.

Rest on his oars? Emerson somewhere has a saying
to the effect that there is something in every success
which makes a greater effort necessary. Though one
may doubt the universal application of this truth, it

was true for Dinwiddy; with results (in our mortal way of looking at these things) to be much deplored.

In the first season in which he flew his broad pennant Dinwiddy made single-handed cruises to the Irish and Brittany coasts, 'uneventfully' (if that word ever could be applied to small-yacht cruising). But for the following year, which was 1938, he planned a single-handed cruise of extra length and special difficulties. Again to Norway—must there not have been some strong Viking strain in the man?—by way of Kiel, Danish east coast, etc., to the great North Fjord. This was an enterprise to test to the uttermost the competence and endurance of the boldest seaman, needless to say. But there were, in this instance, two fateful circumstances. One was the weather, which was rough, wet, cold, sunless, all to an uncommon degree. The other was that Dinwiddy's age was 64.

The following log-entry, when making the S. Norway coast, is all too typical: 'Soon clouds, gathering overhead, burst in a deluge of rain and hail which lasted for twenty-five minutes. Then the wind backed to S.W. and soon freshened. I continued to sail to windward, and it freshened further. At 14.00 I hove-to, double-reefed and shifted staysail, and tried sailing again, but there was too much sea, and I remained hove-to on starboard tack. It blew hard; my flags were as boards, without a sign of flicker.

'By 20.30 the wind had eased and I sailed. The sea was still rough and each wave needed watching. I had drifted a long way seaward, but by dead-reckoning a

course of 300° should make Oskö, the Kristiansand
entrance lighthouse. About two hours later the light
showed just under the lee bow. I was alongside in
Kristiansand at 03.05.'

Svenska had now to work to the westward to round
Lindesnes, Norway's southerly tip, and a Cape Horn
of a place in weather such as Dinwiddy met. Here is
the entry for the first part of the passage; again, all too
typical:

'On the following day I sailed at 09.12 through the
very pretty green-clad islands of the western approach.
Clear of these, the wind was right ahead at W.S.W.
and soon increased to strong. I shifted staysail and
rolled a reef. There was too much sea to sail clear
outside, and I threaded the inner passage, the turning
to windward needed careful watching of the chart in
hard sailing and flying spray.

'The conditions became somewhat strenuous, and I
sailed into Kimlefjorden, and at 14·30 shot alongside
a fishing boat lying at a small quay, finding a perfect
haven under the high hills. At 17.35 I sailed again,
the wind having veered and eased, and by the narrow
inner passage made Mandal at 20.40.'

The very next sentence reads, 'Then it took five
days to round Lindesnes'—*only 15 miles to the westward*!

Dinwiddy sailed much at night on this cruise, and
was necessarily a long time at the helm on numerous
occasions. One spell lasted 30 hours, another 29.
Homeward-bound, he was at one time 42 hours
without sleep. Finally:

'Sailed from Dover with the first of the flood stream down Channel at 06.15. It was a day of very light variable wind, needing much engine. Owers L.V. was made at 21.55. The sky was looking bad, and course was set for Spithead. At midnight the wind came S.W., and the engine was stopped. The wind freshened, with cloud. At 04.05 off Cowes I rolled a reef and remained hove-to for dawn.

'At 05.10 I sailed, the wind very strong. Hove-to off the Beaulieu entrance to make sure of the marks in bad light and conditions. Ran in, and quickly got the anchor and some cable ready and over the side at 06.00. The tide was four hours ebb, and there was almost too much to do in bad weather and with the lee shore close.

'I slept for two hours, and when the flood had made, moved and anchored off Gins.'

Dover to Beaulieu is 115 miles, and before her owner 'slept for two hours' he had been under way for just 24 hours.

Facts of such sort the log states, as always, openly enough; but it was also characteristic that he should say nothing of the resulting fatigue. However, it does seem as though in men of strong will-power fatigue is stowed away, as it were, at compound-interest; the debt being staved off and off . . .

Svenska had left the River Dart on May 9 and returned on August 23, having logged 2,835 miles and visited 62 ports.

'Svenska II' reaches her home port

The closing sentence of the 1938 log had, however, contained this slight concession—or confession: 'And now, after the good sport of single-handed sailing, with three added years, I am intending to get another *Svenska*, a little bigger, to ship a hand to share long watches'.

Svenska II was his last boat, and in her, in the following season, 1939, he made his last cruise.

The new *Svenska*, the lines for which he drew himself, was a roomy 13-tonner built for him in Sweden, where delivery was taken in the early summer, the occasion serving, as was usual with Dinwiddy, for an extensive cruise; nothing shorter, indeed, than a maiden voyage of 2,475 miles, where:

> *Green beneath the headlands*
> *Green rolls the Baltic Sea.*

The waters traversed and the ports visited were, for the most part, the same as by the first *Svenska* and before her by *Eternal Wave*. In short, the cruise occupied 12 weeks, in which space of time *Svenska II* had sailed coastwise to Sandhamn and then to Mariehamn and the Åland Islands. Thence north along the Finnish coast, recrossing the Gulf of Bothnia on the parallel of Umea, from whence down the east coast of Sweden to Stockholm. Passing through the Göta Canal to Gothenburg, she turned north again to explore small ports in the vicinity of the whaling port of Tönsberg, afterwards heading for home by way of the Danish port of Esbjerg, thence coastwise as close as might be to Terschelling, Ymuiden, Ostend, and Dover.

The hand that had been shipped 'to share long night watches' was Mr. J. Kingdom: Eales Bartlett, of the *Eternal Wave* years, having swallowed the anchor (after pretty desperate war experiences afloat) to take charge of the pumping plant of the Brixham U.D.C. But, like Bartlett, Kingdom was 'one of the fine seamen of Brixham', competent, dependable, self-reliant.

This was more than fortunate, for Dinwiddy was often sadly out of sorts. Both he and Kingdom thought the trouble was lumbago, though from the duration and severity of the bouts one must suspect an ailment of more serious kind and deeper source. 'Some days he had a job to do anything', noted Kingdom. 'He got that very tired. I could see he was not himself, because he would leave it to me for hours; not like him.' In particular, Kingdom added, 'He got very bad towards the end of the cruise. You can guess what he was like, because I took the yacht into the Hook of Holland.'.

Again like Bartlett before him, Kingdom deeply admired his owner, for whom also he developed an affection tempered with strong respect.

'One of the best qualities I found in Mr. Dinwiddy was that everything on board had a home of its own, and he made sure that it was always to be found there. And charts; when a day's run was finished, that day's chart was put away. The next being carefully studied for the next day.

'Even when quite laid out you would never see Mr. Dinwiddy untidy—*just like going to Church*!

'I do think the club was everything to him. He was always talking about "The Club".

'He was a grand yachtsman. He had some funny ways at times, but we all have something, I suppose. But I must say he was good to sail with, though you had to be careful just what you said. He was the Country Squire *but good*. And a grand yachtsman who I could not praise too much.'

So Kingdom, so Bartlett ('He was generous, outspoken, strict, and straight'); is it not remarkable, this singleness of testimony from two men particularly and intimately qualified to testify?

Dinwiddy's general condition improved after he had been on shore for a few days. A couple of weeks later, however, war was declared. Whether those dreadful days and the still more dreadful prospect in any way or degree affected or hastened the subsequent deterioration of his health cannot be said with any certainty. Nor did serious illness develop with any alarming suddenness; his condition was rather of increasing debility, the mention of which sometimes escaped him in an occasional letter—'I am so lacking in all that is energy', was one of his patient admissions.

He later underwent an operation. From this, grave as it was, he recovered sufficiently to encourage the hope that he might not only live through the War— but also go to sea again. Alas, it was only his own hopes that were so encouraged. Kingdom, who was trawling through the war years, went to see him at

Stoke Gabriel about this time, to find his owner very weak and sadly changed.

The two men talked of yachting. Dinwiddy outlined the plan for a cruise along the French west coast, pressing the other to prepare for it. But Kingdom, who could not put so much into words, knew it could never be.

It is scarcely possible to depict the scene in words other than Tennyson's *Ulysses*—when the old seafarer calls together his old company and urges on them one last voyage:

> *Something ere the end,*
> *Some work of noble note, may yet be done,*
> *Not unbecoming men that strove with Gods.*
> *The lights begin to twinkle from the rocks:*
> *The long day wanes: the slow moon climbs: the deep*
> *Moans round with many voices. Come, my friends,*
> *'Tis not too late to seek a newer world.*
> *Push off, and sitting well in order smite*
> *The sounding furrows: for my purpose holds*
> *To sail beyond the sunset, and the baths*
> *Of all the western stars, until I die.*
> *It may be that the gulfs will wash us down:*
> *It may be we shall touch the Happy Isles,*
> *And see the great Achilles, whom we know . . .*

But when he died at Stoke Gabriel, on April 20, 1945, Dinwiddy's last voyage had perhaps some different landfall.